SEX & LUST IN TIJUANA:
TRUE SEX STORIES OF THE TJAMIGOS

Professor Zee
Doctor Jim

Editors

She wanted my money and I wanted her body,
so it was a win-win situation!!
-*El Oso*

©2018 The Press of Ill Repute

All rights reserved. No part of this publication may be reproduced, distributed or transmitted in any form or by any means, including photocopying, recording, or other electronic or mechanical methods, without the prior written permission of the publisher, except in the case of brief quotations embodied in critical reviews and certain other noncommercial uses permitted by copyright law.

The Press of Ill Repute, Tijuana

Front cover photo by dubsack;back cover photo by IMinTJ

For wholesale or other inquiries, contact tjamigosbook@gmail.com

Sex and Lust in Tijuana: True Sex Stories of the TJAmigos/Professor Zee and Doctor Jim, editors. —1st ed.
ISBN 978-1-946341-01-3 (print), ISBN 978-1-946341-02-0 (digital)

Dedicated to all the men and women who seek information about keeping sex workers and themselves safe in Tijuana.

We believe that no country or culture should have the power to take away any person's consensual ability to work their own way. Consensual sex work is not a myth and in many places on this planet it is alive, accepted, and thriving.

Recent anti-trafficking legislation has forced a number of educational sites concerning information for consensual sex to shut down. This publication is designed to help eliminate many of the falsehoods associated with this legislation. Firstly, consensual sex work is NOT sex trafficking. It is a complete myth that everyone in the sex trade is there by force or coercion of a violent nature. The truth is that sex workers in countries like Mexico see sex work as their way out of poverty. Of the many women that choose to sell themselves, it is often economic necessity that drives them. There are many women who are of lower economic means that are unable to get jobs and are generally the only breadwinner in the family. An economic reality is that there is a need to find income for them and their children for basic needs like food, clothing, housing, education, and healthcare. Sex work is a viable and significant financial employment opportunity for many.

CONTENTS

Introduction
Doctor Jim, Editor . . . . *i*

Glossary
Acronyms, Spanish, Other Terms . . . . *iii*

The Ol' Back and Forth: Five Days of Debauchery
Senojyllib *1*

A New Low
Pastor G Spot *14*

Fusion Lets His Guard Down
Fusion *19*

Trip Trilogy
TJ500 . . . . *25*

Fast Times on a Wild Wednesday Night
El Oso *30*

An Evil Force Overtook Me
Catfish *33*

Another First Timer's Report
Georgie Orgie *36*

First Trip to Adelita
Epithumia *42*

I Can't Remember Her Name
ZePequeno *45*

HK Chica Has a Real Talent
Dr. F *48*

RyGuy and The Homeboys' First Trip to TJ
RyGuy *51*

No One Here Gets Out Alive
Kendricks *54*

The Freakiest Bargirl I Ever Met
SecretAmigoX *58*

Bullshitting the Bullshitter: PLM Pulls the Ultimate Scam
Maverick. *62*

A FOB Slobbed My Knob
ElNique *69*

I Was Robbed!
SMD *71*

Maddog's Adventure with Kamala
Maddog *87*

Beautiful ROB Does Detention
Trolleyman *93*

Forbidden Fruit
Kendricks *96*

Tania Sucks Maddog
Maddog *101*

Stay Flexible
Doh *105*

Lunchtime Mission
CraigfromSD *112*

Experiment in Madness
Paco *115*

Code Name: Crying Game
C-Diddy *118*

TJ Hookers: This Is Their Scam
Various *122*

How I Spent $400 and Got No Sex
Mad Ogre *128*

The Goal
Ninja23 . . . . *133*

Don't You Remember Me?
Erip *138*

All in the Family
Byron *142*

I Thought It Was Love Until…
Various *145*

A Week in Tijuana
Mic *149*

Sex in the City
AsianMovieLover *166*

Did Grandma Ever Take it Up the Ass? Ask Grandpa!
Amo *171*

Good and Bad Report
Buttman *174*

Fear & Self-Loathing in Tijuana
Matiz *177*

Like a Virgin, Yo!
Erip *194*

At the Mercy of the Beast
Kendricks *202*

Acknowledgements
Editors *209*

Introduction

DOCTOR JIM, EDITOR

The TJAmigos are a diverse crew, made up of men from all walks of life. Young, old, middle-aged, skinny, fat, regular-sized, good-looking, average Joes, and from every race and socioeconomic bracket there is. The Amigos are bound by their love of pussy and the allure of Tijuana, which is home to Zona Norte, a world famous redlight district. The Zona Norte has always had working ladies; from its earliest days with the now-shuttered Molino Rojo to Adelita to Chicago Club to the current hotspot—the multi-level and still-growing Hong Kong Gentlemen's Club with lots of other bars and chicas in between on the streets.

TJAmigos was a discussion forum website started in 2003 for the men who frequented Tijuana to be able to swap stories and share information with each other. It became a brotherhood of sorts where the guys (known as mongers) would not only share stories but give each other support and advice on all sorts of topics and quandaries.

Before TJAmigos closed down in early 2018 in response to the nebulous SESTA/FOSTA legislation in the United States, it had more than 25,000 members who had created more than 1.5 million posts.

Fortunately, the website was archived offline. In the summer of 2018, Professor Zee and I undertook the task of combing through all these posts from over fifteen years to bring you a peek into the redlight district of Tijuana. With some of the stories, we have also included comments from the Amigos.

Picking through all those posts and deciding which stories to include was harder than finding a true virgin in a whorehouse, but we did it!

¡PROVECHO!

(p/s - The glossary that follows this introduction is for all the hobby specific acronyms and terms you'll run across in the stories…)

GLOSSARY

ACRONYMS

AB – Adelita Bar

AMP – Asian massage parlor

ATF – All-time favorite

ATM – Ass to mouth

BB – Bareback (no condom)

BBBJ – Bareback blowjob

BBFS – Bareback full service

BF – Bar fine (Fee paid to the club to get a chica dismissed before her shift ends)

BG – Bar girl

BH – Beverly Hills (club on Revolución, now closed)

BJ – Blowjob

BLS – Ball licking and sucking

BT – Bar Tropical

CBJ – Covered blowjob (with condom)

CC – Chicago Club

CFS – Covered full service, sex with condom

CG – Cowgirl: girl on top facing you

CIM – Cum in mouth

COF – Cum on face; also called a **facial**

DATY – Dining at the Y (eating pussy)

DATO – Dining at the O (eating ass)

DFE – Dead fish experience (meaning she just lays there)

DFK – Deep French kissing; also **LFK** – light French kissing

DT – Deep throat

FB – Facebook

FOB – Fresh off the bus (chica very new to the scene)

FS – Full service (sex and blowjob)

GFE – Girlfriend Experience (great sex – includes: **FS, BJ, DATY**, not a clock watcher, **DFK**, treats you like her boyfriend)

GND – Girl Next Door

HJ – Hand job – a manual/hand release

HK – Hong Kong Club

LC – Las Chavelas

LE – Law enforcement

MILF – Mom I'd like to fuck;

GLOSSARY

also **GILF** – Grandma I'd like to fuck

P4P – Pay for pussy

PLM – Pathetic loser monger (Guy who falls for a sex worker and gets taken advantage of financially in a big way by her)

PSE – Porn-star experience (Opposite of **GFE**, but an incredibly good time. So good it was like being in a porn movie)

MP – Massage parlor

MSOG – Multiple shots on goal; multiple releases

OTC – Off the clock/outside the club

RJ – Rimjob. rimming. Lick an asshole

ROB – Rip-off Bitch. Chica who steals money or promises sexual services she doesn't provide

SC – Strip club

SG – Street girl (also **paradita** – Spanish for standing girl)

SO – Significant other

STD – Sexually transmitted disease

TLN – Toda la noche (All night long or "All–nighter")

TR – Trip report

TS – Transsexual

TV – Transvestite

TG – Transgender

TGTBT – Too good to be true

TJ – Tijuana

TJA – TJ Amigos

TOFTT – Take one for the team (being the first to try something out and report back)

UTR – Under the radar (used when a chica isn't advertised but is still working)

WTF? – What the fuck?

YMMV – Your mileage may vary

ZN – The Zona Norte, also called **Zona, zone,** or **LZ**

SPANISH

Con condón – With condom

Sin condón – Without condom

Cambio – Change. "No cambio," means "I don't need my change back"; also: a place to exchange money, "What cambio has the best rate right now?"

Chica – Girl

GLOSSARY

Cita – Appointment

Cuarto – Hotel room

Culo - Ass

Ficha – Ticket that BGs get when you buy them a drink (also used to refer to the small beer/drink the chica receives)

Fichera – Chica that only drinks and dances for fichas

Flaca/flakita – Thin (see also **spinner**)

Gabacho – Caucasian, similar to Gringo

Gorda/gordita – Overweight chica

Güera – Light-skinned Mexican girl

La Linéa – The line (border crossing)

Mesero – Waiter (**mesera** – waitress)

Morena – Mexican girl with dark (brown) skin

Novia – Girlfriend (**novio** – boyfriend)

Padrote – A pimp, husband, or boyfriend who lives off the earnings of a prostitute

Por favor – Please

Pinche gringo – A pejorative term meaning something like "damn Gringo"; sometimes used jokingly

Propina – Tip for service

Puta – Whore (offensive, don't say this to the chicas!)

Regalo – Gift

Ropa – Clothing

Rubia – Mexican girl with blonde hair (She may or may not also be a güera – a light-skinned Mexican girl)

Tacones – High heels

Tienda – Small store

Toda la noche – All night

Tollechero – A guy that cleans the rooms in the short–time hotels

OTHER TERMS

Alley – Callejon Coahuila. An alley between Constitución and Niños Heroes, filled with street girls

Agency – A company that manages calls, bookings, and advertising for a group of providers/escorts

Analingus – Licking anus

GLOSSARY

Asian Cowgirl – Girl on top, squatting

Bait and switch – Person who shows up is a different one than advertised

Bareback – Without condom

Blue pill – Viagra (also called Vitamin V)

Butterface – Everything looks good, but her face

Civvie – Chica who is not a sexworker (also written as **civie**)

Cover – Condom

Facial – Cumming on partner's face

Greek – Anal sex

Hat – Condom

Hobby – Patronizing prostitutes

Hobbyist – Man who patronizes prostitutes

Kriko – Crystal meth

Mish – Missionary position

Missionary – Man on top, girl on her back

Monger – Man who purchases sex from a prostitute; from the word "whoremonger"; also as a verb: "He's mongered all over southeast Asia."

OXXO – Convenience store chain in Mexico; there are hundreds of them around TJ

Rev/Revo – Avenida Revolución

Rimming – Analingus

Russian – Fucking a chica between the breasts

Spinner – Very petite, thin girl

Starfish – Chica who just spreads her legs for you and does nothing else

Tossing salad – Analingus

Walker – Chica without a regular working spot, generally without ID and without a health card; also called **freelancer**

WhatsApp – Phone app used in Mexico for texting and calls, works over WiFi

¡Bienvenidos

a Tijuana,

Amigo!

The Ol' Back and Forth: Five Days of Debauchery

SENOJYLLIB

Your first entry into Hong Kong is like the first sip of an ice cold beer after a hot day of work, going through the turnstiles at Disneyland when you are nine, seeing a great friend for the first time in a decade, or walking into your favorite Irish pub on Saint Patrick's morning; it is a moment of overwhelming joy and happiness. I stood looking, ignoring los meseros, and just absorbed the club. The lights! The music! The ladies! I almost cried; I was so happy as my nostrils flared and my muscles clenched. I closed my eyes and then opened them as I looked towards the sky only to see scores of more beautiful women. *Oh yeah...*

So my plan, having not eaten too much due to a half day of travel, was to check into Cascadas, and then take it easy while searching for my first amiga favorita of the trip. That plan lasted about three minutes after checking in at Cascadas, walking downstairs, and going over to Tropical where I just wanted to settle in, enjoy my 2x1 Tecates and continue to slowly acclimate (with plans to hit MonteCarlo for an omelet ASAP). But along with my Tecates, the mesero brought over a young brunette, who I wouldn't describe as a classic flakita. But she was young, fresh, full of energy, and had legs up to her gorgeous eyes. She was proud of her body as she should be, and explained in broken English how she worked out to keep her 19-year-old body so toned. She had an ass like an onion, and was easily an eight by anybody's standard, however, not really my type. *But oh my God, what a body!* She just kept nibbling on my neck and ears while lightly stroking my cock and balls. And she was ficha'ing me at full bore so I felt obligated to keep up with her furious cerveza pace.

I think most men would rate her a nine, but I'm more of a big titted blonde man. So at some point, I promised el mesero and mi amiga that I would return tomorrow for more.

I crossed over to Dulce Gabanna and parted the heavy velvet curtains to reveal a very different club from when I last visited. It was much, much busier and the girls didn't seem as new. They seem more hardened (not as in toned but as in "I've been working in La Zona for some time now"), albeit every one of them was young. I sat near a Mexican fellow with a big grin while I waited for a mesero. It was actually so busy that I wasn't bombarded with meseros vying for my money. My Mexican buddy handed me a cold cerveza from his bucket, and I returned the favor after purchasing a bucket of my own. This immediately brought over two ladies, a blonde for me and a brunette for mi amigo. So now I'm two hours into my night of taking it easy and ten beers deep on an empty stomach.

Things started to get fuzzy from that point on, but here's what I know for sure. Armando and I went to at least two more bars, including Gold Palace where there was some sort of incident between me and a girl. I'm pretty sure it happened in the VIP, when I was insisting on a blowjob sin condom and she was insisting on a blowjob con condom. The next day, the doorman spoke with me about it, kind of shaking his head asking if I remembered last night.

"Yeah, of course, why?" I reply, not quite sure of what he was talking about. He said something about "...you and the girl, upstairs, you remember?" I looked him in the eye and asked, "I'm okay to come here? Sí o no?" He nodded his head yes, gave me a smile and a handshake as I walked past.

Back to Saturday night/Sunday morning, after being dissatisfied with my BJ at Gold Palace, I ventured into Las Chavelas to find a woman who I could take it out on. I found a 30-ish brunette with breeder hips and gigantic tits. Not ugly, but not the type who is going to have a line of clients waiting for her services. It wasn't long before Lucia and I agreed on fifty dollars and were upstairs in Cascadas while I was getting my blowjob sin condom and getting smothered by my lady who finished me off cowgirl style.

After getting rid of her along with a five-dollar tip, I hopped a cab back to Garita de Otay to cross the border back to the US and get to my US hotel.

So much for taking it easy on my first night…

Day Two

Hungover as hell on Sunday, I exchanged a bunch of dollars into pesos and returned to Mexico and my hotel room down in La Zona. I stocked up on snacks and drinks from OXXO and the Tecate store on the corner, stashed my pesos in the safe, grabbed a cheese omelet in MonteCarlo, and headed out to explore. Even knowing that it was mid-afternoon on a Sunday, La Zona seemed quiet. Chicago Club was empty (and was empty the four or five times I poked my head in throughout the trip). La Gloria was a bit busy, but I couldn't find anybody attractive to me in there. Play Boy, Hacienda, and Valentina were all dead.

I made a loop through Adelita, but found it to be very cold and uninviting. Over my five days in La Zona Norte, I had to have made twelve runs through Adelita and never even bought a beer. Sure, there were many attractive women, but not many flakitas, and I caught a certain hardened vibe from most of the ladies. They were certainly smiling, ready and willing, but I just didn't feel "it." Some of this may have come from my allegiance to Cascadas and its affiliates because I was staying there; regardless, I never found a lady to take upstairs from Adelita over my five days. Or even sit down for a drink with. That's quite different from prior trips.

With that said, I would still say that six out of ten girls in Adelita would probably rate as the best looking girl in almost any US strip club at any given time. They are very pretty, but equally tough. I grabbed a younger girl (probably 22-ish) from Las Chavelas to take upstairs. By no means did she sport Adelita-quality looks, but man, she had a gorgeous smile, deep dark eyes that seemed almost innocent, and a beautiful set of natural C cups that just bounced like they only can when they are real and young. After a couple of fichas, we agreed on sixty American. She was simply wonderful, there was no clock watching, and it was a true GFE by any standard. I walked her downstairs afterwards, and retired to sleep.

Later, after showering and feeling refreshed, I took in the sights of Hong Kong. Finally, I returned to Chavelas and immediately fell into the arms of my 30-year-old friend from Sunday. We had a couple of fichas, made out for 20 minutes, and went upstairs for one of the most fun, relaxed, sensuous 90 minutes of my life. I was in complete bliss, tossed a hundred dollars in her purse, and once again walked my lady back downstairs to Las Chavelas before retiring for another nap.

My headache was gone, my testicles were drained, and I slept like a newborn with no alarms, deadlines, wife, child, mother, boss, client, or anybody to be worried about. I had found what I was looking for. Peace.

DAY THREE

With no external windows, I wondered what time it was when I awoke from my slumber. If I had to guess, I would have said eight in the morning, but after taking a shower and heading out of the room, I discovered it was early afternoon..

A mesera sat me down in some bar (I'm not sure which) and

brought me a young lady with a body that could only be described as "tight." Not really toned like she worked out, but you know, tight—no fat, supple curves, A cups, maybe five feet tall. She wasn't really pretty (but not ugly), but her body was so fresh and new, I was in lust.

After a few fichas and some agreed upon price that wasn't a lot, we went to Cascadas where I just immersed myself with this shy quiet girl. There was no way she had children, and while she was a relatively inexperienced lay, she was incredibly tight in all regards. Upon return to the bar and our booth, the DJ just looks at this 50-year-old fat balding gringo and his thin supple 19-year-old novia and screams, "WHAT THE FUCK!?!?!" over the speakers. Not once, but a second time while pointing at us, and then a third time as he walked over and kind of held us up with his outstretched arms screaming "What the fuck???"

It was great.

I ducked out soon after because it was now getting dark. I wandered around the various bars, once again starting to get pretty drunk. And once again sporting an empty stomach with the exception of alcohol. I finally ended up in the arms of a 26-year-old at La Malquerida that was just my type: blonde, sporting about ten extra pounds and most of those in her chest. She said she had four kids by four papis and doesn't want a novio, that she just loves sexo. When she opened my second beer bottle with her teeth, I fell in immediate love. I would have liked to have let her ficha me as long as she wanted, but I started to feel a bit drained so I bid farewell.

I wandered up Constitución, which was dumb given my drunken state. I surfed the smaller bars off Ave Revo and ended up hanging out with two gorditas, one of whom took a major liking to me. I was hammered and she was taking full advantage of my drunken state. She weighed an easy 250 and was on me like a cheap suit.

We ended up taking a cab back to La Zona, going to one or two bars, and then heading up to my room where she completely molested my drunken Viagra'd ass. I thought the stripper pole in my room was going to get torn off its hinges, but was more than glad to confirm the existence of a va-jay-jay between those legs during her pole work, and then this girl started licking my asshole like it was a lollipop, just for starters.

I passed out, and when I woke up she was gone (except for a pair of earrings). My pants pockets had been emptied of probably $100. She nicely left me with $10 in my pocket, and thankfully never found the key to my safe (or more than likely, never realized there was a safe in the room).

Once I got my bearings straight, I headed back to the US to recuperate from that debacle. No issues, and I continued back to my room to try to forget about the gordita who robbed me of my Benjamin the night before.

DAY FOUR

For whatever reason, I was convinced it was Monday as I headed back to Mexico on Tuesday. As I got up and walked back to Mexico, it was Monday in my mind. For sure. 100%, it is Monday. So with nothing to do that day, I wandered around Revo to kill some time, went back to my room, then strolled around La Zona, and ended up in Play Boy. I put $50 in the slot machine thing, which attracted a few dancers because to do so meant getting two Solo-sized cups full of two-peso coins.

We all joined in for a massive ficha and slot machine-palooza. Playing games where you pick a box, if it has a key, you move up the ladder to pick the next box, *ding-ding-ding-ding-ding...* yeah!!!! Then a game like a slot machine, where if you win, you can choose to double up, then some buzzer goes off... high fives for everybody, yeah!!!!!

Each girl was the queen of this game or that. *Don't pick the box with bomb in it!* Or *get the tools that match to open the thingy to win!* I don't know… All I knew was that I had thrown fifty bucks in this thing that was spewing out two-peso coins and we were stacking them in stacks of ten that started to overtake the corner of the bar. We were paying for drinks and chips and whatever with stacks of two-peso coins. Like "Three fichas!" "Okay. That's 300 pesos." "Bueno. Here are fifteen stacks of coins."

I convinced a relatively shy blonde (yes… a blonde!!! If you haven't already figured it out, me likey blondes) to join in and we made room for a stool for her next to me. She couldn't miss on the "pick a higher card" game, and she and I were high fiving every time she won, which led to a kiss when she won, which led to her sitting on my lap. Eventually the machine had 2000 credits, which is the maximum ("CALL ATTENDANT"). It was a riot. The blonde, another girl, and I retired to upstairs for some heavy petting with my dick to celebrate.

Then the blonde worked out the details and paid the manager whatever out of her pocket (it didn't look like more than a fifty-peso bill) so we could leave and go to Cascadas. The other girl from upstairs didn't like this, but as the manager explained, "She's upset but I told her she made nine fichas, so she should not be crying." It was a crazy run on that machine, because if you figure four or five girls times eight or nine fichas each, that's got to be $200 on fichas alone before my drinks, tips, or the money I took with me at the end.

I took the blonde to Cascadas and we had a good time, nothing spectacular, but a good fuck. She asked if we could go to La Perla for dinner, and I said sure. We were warming up to each other, but as dinner was winding down, I realized it was Tuesday, not Monday!

It was already six o'clock and I had tickets for a seven o'clock baseball game in downtown San Diego. My date (that's what it felt like) begged me to go to Plaza Santa Cecilia with her instead of making her return to the bar, but I sadly told her I was already late in terms of getting back to the US. I think it would have been a heck of a time if we had went out for the evening, and kind of wish we did.

I cabbed it back to Otay, crossed the border, grabbed a cab on the US side and had the cabbie wait for me while I got the tickets from my room. He drove me to the trolley, and I made the fourth inning at Petco.

As I took the trolley back to San Ysidro after the game, I wondered what would have happened if I had stayed in TJ and taken my blonde friend out for the evening. But I'm happy I got to see Petco Park and a little bit of baseball. Man, I was enjoying life to its fullest.

When I got back to La Zona, I headed straight to La Malquerida, where the 26-year-old from the previous night promised to be waiting just for me. I was aghast to discover she had found another man to occupy her time!

Nonetheless, I sat down and was quickly introduced to a drop-dead gorgeous raven-haired flakita with perfect legs, a perfect ass, beautiful C cup tits, and a set of lips made for sucking cock. Naomi was her name. She was, by far, one of the best-looking girls I had seen during the entire trip. She had more energy than I've ever imagined. I'd bet she was on something. Or probably a combination of a couple of things. Within a few fichas, I agreed to take her to Cascadas for $80. Then the doorman wanted a bar fine of like 25 bucks, and the mesero insisted that I buy a bucket of beer. With the exception of the $80 that I agreed to give Naomi, I was getting massively screwed. But nothing was going to get in the way of me getting this girl in my room. Period.

Naomi was a freak in bed. Four fingers in the front, two in the back, riding like no tomorrow, crazy gorgeous woman who looks three times better naked than dressed up... I still can't get over this girl who just wants to be violated while watching porno. I don't think she has any limits. I think she needs a guy (or a couple of guys) with much bigger dicks than mine.

After a half hour, she stopped and negotiated for more. I gave her 2000 pesos (total) and I said no more time limits. She was fine with that. If I had tried to really keep up with her, without a doubt, I would have had a heart attack. I walked her back to the bar, retired to my room, stacked some beer cans and bottles up against the door, and went to sleep.

Day Five

Wednesday, a sad day. Because it was my last day...

I woke up in the afternoon and headed back towards Revo to hit some bars before I skipped back to the US for an hour or so, then on to my final night of debauchery in TJ.

Before I went back to my room in the US, in the Mariachi Bar, I was approached by a non-pro (I think) who was in her late 20s (I think) who was a solid six right then and probably an eight in her day. Her nicest asset was a gorgeous rack that seemed natural (I think). She asked me for a drink, which I gladly bought. She received a ficha that was immediately paid to her in cash, which is the first time that I've seen a ficha happen in that fashion instead of a ticket. She insisted that I dance. She made me smile. She made me happy. She apologized for not wearing makeup or nice clothes or big shoes because she had stopped in for only one beer. I told her I had to leave, but would return in two hours and be happy to see her again even if she was still not wearing makeup, fancy clothes, or big shoes.

Bidding her adieu, I knew she would not be there when I returned. I jetted back to the US to attend to a bit of work and to pack for Thursday morning's departure (just in case I got caught up in something that might require that I stick around in Mexico until the last possible second). I showered up and changed. Aside from my next day's clothing, everything was pretty much packed and ready to roll as if I were leaving right then and there. I left the maid a tip primarily because she honored the DO NOT DISTURB sign that had hung on my door for five consecutive days.

A bit later than promised, I returned to the Mariachi Bar. My amiga was there, talking with another man, whom she introduced me to. Then, to my surprise, he left. She told me she thought I wasn't going to return. We had a few drinks.

Just as I was thinking that I should bounce her out of there to another bar, she suggested we go somewhere else for a couple more. We stopped in the Caliente Casino to try our luck. She insisted blackjack was her game, and she wanted to wait for an open seat at the one table that was going. When we couldn't get on that table, she convinced the floor man to open another. I bought her $100 in chips and $100 for me. I explained to her that her $100 stake was mine, but anything that she won beyond that was hers to keep.

I then watched in horror as she tried as hard as possible to prove that she is the World's Worst Blackjack Player. With extreme indignation and a righteous attitude. Giving me a glaring woman-stare when I suggested she might not want to split her sevens against a dealer's ten. Or not stand on a twelve versus an ace. She doubled down on a fourteen! She politely explained that I was making her nervous by offering suggestions regarding her play.

Every move she made, she thought out to an extreme level—analyzing all the cards on the table, thinking it through and then… her decision as the rest of the table waited with bated breath to see what she would do. The tension was Shakespearean.

Inevitably, the dealer would curiously confirm what she was asking him to do, and she would insist that he act upon her wishes. He began to dutifully look to me for confirmation, to which I could only shrug my shoulders and nod. Her actions oftentimes produced winces, painful moans or "ooohhs" from the other players at the table as if they had just witnessed a baby deer being run over by a truck. In a US casino, she would have driven all of the other players off the table.

After losing her $100 and trying to lose most of mine, we

departed for Caesar's for dinner, but only after buying her a dress (that I negotiated down to $20) from one of those Revo stores that sells everything from wrestling masks to apparently dinner dresses. It was really neat to have her ask me to block the street view as she strutted to the back of the store to take off her shirt (further exposing her gorgeous chest) and change into her new dress that fit her perfectly. She looked stunning in red with her hair down.

In the restaurant, her manners and class were perfect. As the mariachi band played a couple of romantic songs she picked, the "six" that I had met at the bar five hours earlier was transforming into an "eight" before my eyes. It was one of the nicest dinner dates that I have ever been on. But in the end, we both talked about needing to take a nap.

So I'm thinking, "Great. I just dropped a few hundred bucks on this good-looking woman, who now is talking about taking a nap with me. Sounds like a pretty good finish to a fun five days in Mexico."

We're lazily walking down Revolución towards the arch, hand in hand, arm in arm, her head on my shoulder. We decided to go to Bar Nelson (which happens to be attached to a hotel, wink, wink), and on the way she wants to stop in the OXXO. Who am I to say no to a soda or snack for my beautiful senorita? She then picks out a $100 smartphone. I'm like no!

She says, "I have no phone, I will text you every day."

I said, "I'll give you my burner phone."

She looks at me with that blackjack stare and pouty lips and says, "You have the money, why you no buy me my phone?"

I looked her in the eyes and with a coy smile, I said, "I'm not buying a phone."

We left, but now there's no hand holding. There's no arm in arm. There's no head on shoulder. She needed to use el baño, so we go back to Casino Caliente, and then return down the street, growing more distant from each other by the step.

At 3rd Street, she starts to pull me left towards Constitución. I said, "Where are you going?" and she says "A shortcut!" I said no shortcuts for me as she insisted and then she continued down the street.

Oh well! I bee-lined it to Bar Nelson for one drink, and then cabbed it back to La Zona.

I ended up back at La Malquerida and had a word with the doorman, who looks like a gruff Italian from *The Sopranos*. I asked him if there would be a bar fine if I decided to take a lady to Cascadas (which is an affiliated hotel). It seemed like he was taken aback and tried to intimidate me a bit by calling the mesero who carried our bucket of beer the night before.

He asked, "What are you saying? Is there a problem?" while the two of them stood at the doorway with their arms crossed sporting their meanest faces they could muster.

I calmly and politely said, "Why no! There is no problem! I'm just asking a question. If I bring a lady from this bar to my hotel where I am staying, which is Cascadas, will there be a bar fine?"

They spoke for 20 seconds in Spanish and then replied, "No, there is no bar fine."

I then asked, "Do I have to buy a girl a bucket?"

They spoke again for five seconds and then said, "No, nothing except paying him *(pointing at the doorman)* five dollars."

I clarified this one final time with a smile on my face, confirming that if I wished to take a girl from the bar to Cascadas that would entail a five dollar fee to the doorman and nothing more. We shook hands, I thanked them, put my arm around the mesero, and asked for a Tecate as I walked in the bar.

I was sad not to find my chesty blonde friend who could open a beer bottle with her teeth, but was recognized immediately by the flakita from a night before. I was a little concerned that she might feel a bit defiled by our escapades after she sobered up from the night before. But there was no animosity on her part towards me.

Just the opposite, as a matter of fact. Or perhaps she hadn't sobered up in the last 24 hours. I don't know, but once we sat down in a booth, she wanted my fingers up her ass and some hyper-aggressive pussy jamming, which got her wet as fuck once again. There was a younger fellow watching us from his booth across the way who was mesmerized by her aggressive pulsing to the music on my fist and fingers. I'd again offer that she was fucked up big time and might suggest that if she were to go out dancing that it would involve glow sticks and lollipops along with whatever else she was into (just a guess).

After four or five fichas with Naomi, I decided to leave and make a final loop through La Zona with her as my "Plan B" if I couldn't find something different (variety being the spice of life, and me not being sure I could handle another delivery of a craze-driven pussy and ass attack).

Around 2am, I found a 22-year-old dirty blonde 9 with natural B cups in Hong Kong who agreed to join me for some fun upstairs in my room for $70. I was drunk, tired, and overall just shot. I was having trouble shooting a load and maintaining a woody. But she was a true trooper refusing to give up, blowing me like a champion and finally finishing me off by hand—with a nice attitude and smile on her face—despite my embarrassing shortcomings.

I walked her back downstairs and returned to clean up my room. I hung the two earrings that the gordita ratera left behind on the wire Oriental tree fixture in the room. I tossed everything else out except for a small pack of Oreos, and I left a nice tip for the maid that included the unopened pint of Bacardi. I checked out, got my $20 deposit back for the key to the safe and the remote, and asked if I could keep my key as a souvenir.

Well before sunrise, I was back at Garita de Otay with a pack of six Oreos as my declaration of the only thing that I was returning from Mexico with… I hope.

A New Low

PASTOR G SPOT

I was standing outside Nikki's when Lorena Lopez steamed towards me, swinging her titties under her slightly too big sheer blouse. All I wanted was an hour of fluffing from her, but she offered a lot more in whispered tones as we walked to the Hotel Paris. As I am laying on my back on what must have been a bedbug infested blanket, looking up yet again at the biggest hole I have ever seen in a ceiling, I wondered what it would take to get out of the room when there was no door knob and I had to really push on the door to close it. I would give Ms. Lopez a 6 on her blow job technique and a 1 on ball sucking. She swears I was her first and I totally believe her.

About 15 minutes in, she starts looking around while bobbing her head on my dick and wiggling her ass. She grabs a brown paper bag she had left on the bed, pulls out a plastic bag with a pan dulce in it, pulls out the baked good, and opens out the plastic bag and pees in it. Even though I was shocked, *shocked I say*, the gentleman in me pulled a handiwipe out and handed it to her.

Ms. Lopez has had breast reduction surgery that has left her right breast senseless. Her left nipple is very sensitive to make up for it and she rubbed one out as I sucked it.

Ms. Lopez had me fuck her in about four different positions, and at one point asked me to stick it in her culo and finish in five minutes. She told me she could not take more than five minutes of butt fucking. I did not finish and will not repeat.

Next up was Wendy at the Eduardo. Nice attitude, looks, perky A cups and lots of suction power. Allowed me to massage her g-spot with two fingers while I thumbed her clit and she sucked me off and licked my nuts. I will repeat.

Perla just south of the ICC was last today. Cute face but a paunch like a pregnant Labrador Retriever that I did not notice. Does she wear a corset? I will not repeat.

Girls = 700 pesos
Parking = 8 dollars
2 tacos = 2.5 dollars
Coke at OXXO where both cashiers are gay = 1 dollar
Dried out cigar from Adelita = 1 dollar
Hotels = 170 pesos

Amigo Commentary

Moose: I think the nastiest was when a guy here posted that a girl took a shit on the bed while he was fucking her in mish at the AB hotel.

BigDick: Epic TR, but know this: we mongers although we skirt along the bottom of society, despised by some, hated by others, associating with the scuzz of society so committing sundry acts of perversion can ALWAYS go lower.

ZePechulo: She pisses in a bag during a BBBJ, and you won't repeat? Why did you even continue? I would have ended it right there. That isn't gross; it is downright repulsive.

DavezPlace: Agree 100%. Soon as she told me I couldn't drink the bag's contents, I'd be up and out the door!

OffTango: At least she didn't eat her baked goods while being a starfish. Great thread, if I could like it twice, I would.

Edit: On second thought, I had to come back and ask: Why did she even bother with a bag?

Pastor G Spot: Ms. Lopez was on meth or suffers from ADHD or a perhaps little of both. It seemed that her attention span was about 90 seconds and I had to remind her to keep sucking me about eight times in the first 15 minutes. The first time she tried to climb on me, I told her, "Keep sucking, baby." When she tried to give me a two-fisted handjob, I told her "Keep sucking, honey." On the 7th or 8th time, I had to give her my raised eyebrow I will not pay you shit look as I said "Keep sucking."

After she started looking around, she stopped the bobbing action but did not uncouple off my wiener as she grabbed for the plastic bag. It wasn't until I saw a golf ball of piss form at the bottom of the bag that I realized what the fuck she was doing. I didn't stare at her pissing, but instead, I looked back up at the hole in the ceiling and realized that I had hit an all-time low.

She brought the bag between the bed and just under the window and I was not sure if she was going to drop it along the wall, fling it out the window, or somehow get it on me. She tied a knot in the bag and put it back into the brown paper bag all the time with her mouth on my dick.

Hooky: And you are confirming that you didn't have to pay her extra for that?

ClubDano: That's multitasking for ya. Pissing and blowing. Great read. And you're a better man than me... no way I could've kept wood.

Pastor G Spot: I didn't pay any extra for the piss in the bag, the rub-one-out-while-sucking-on-her-working-nipple, or request to fuck her in the culo. As I was giving it to her in doggie, she licked the front of her fingers, pulled forward so I slipped out, and she reached back between her legs and either rubbed her anus or stuck a quick finger or two up her butt, and she told me to fuck her in the culo and finish in five minutes. This provider does not upsell.

ZePechulo: Just curious, what does Ms. Lopez look like? Is she attractive or not so much?

SMD: So what are her work hours?

Pastor G Spot: About 5'1", 115 pounds, dark hair, no makeup at all, brown eyes. Daytime. Hope that helps.

For the most part, I don't care what a fluffer looks like. I only see the back of their head, but on the 1-10 scale for walkers, a very generous 5. Out on the street, I was looking through the armholes of her blouse staring at her aureoles and nipples while I was offering her my simple menu of dick and ball sucking for an hour for 300 pesos, pay later. Her white cotton blouse was very sheer and because she was facing east, the morning sun really lit up her chi-chis. She looked much better with her clothes on.

As far as keeping wood: I had 25mgs of V at 9am and 90mgs of V at 9:30am.

Prairie Dog: The mannerisms of some of the folks in TJ are a little different from ours. I used to see this stripper that became like a part-time GF because I was going every weekend. She worked at Play Boy and would leave with me and spend the night at whatever hotel I could get my hands on.

One night, we got this little shack of a room that had a bathroom but no door. She went right in and let a river flow pretty much right in front of me. I was shocked, but even worse I had to take a massive dump and remember, the bathroom had no door. I tried finding a restroom outside of the hotel and failed. I ended up taking a massive noisy dump while she was basically sitting right next to me on the bed; I mean, no big deal in TJ. Then I fucked the shit out of her and had a great night. She stopped stripping when I stopped visiting as often. I still miss her pretty face and the GF treatment.

BigDick: In my life, I have faced down an armed gunman and I say without braggadocio I am really not afraid of anyone…probably Irish stupidity. BUTT (and a site about gorgeous Latinas always has a BIG BUTT), I honestly fear squeezing the pumpkin, dropping a watermelon, or as some may prosaically call it: The Public Dump.

Fusion Lets His Guard Down

FUSION

So first of all, I had a great time with an old chica friend tonight. Then it was time to go and that's where I screwed up. When the night was done, I realized I had no money to get back in a taxi, so I walked, feeling sober enough to watch my back against male rateros… except I didn't count on the female rateros to get me.

As I was walking past the 7-11, a female ratero started to follow me and ask for change. Her name was Erika. I apologized and told her that I had nothing to give her which was the truth. She persisted and said that she just wanted to walk with me cause she rarely had any human contact, but I thought that was weird because she also said that she grew up in TJ all her life and wasn't deported like I thought she was.

She continued to follow me, telling me her sob story in perfect English, until we got to the ramps that usually had vendors during the daytime. That's when she started to rub my dick. She wasn't a bad looking woman, and she smelled like she bathed regularly because she smelled like shampoo, so my dick couldn't help but get hard. It was such a turn on because it was just me and her, in this dark walkway leading to Chaparral as she whispered telling me that all she wanted was my dick as she stroked it.

I told her that I didn't want to be jumped by her homies with whatever clarity I had left, all while she stroked me saying that all she wanted was "this", as she squeezed my cock. She insisted that we would go to an area she knew because she wanted to blow me.

I said no to that but suggested that we go a random dark corner that I saw (yes, I know—stupid), which wasn't hard because there were so many dark corners we could hide in at that time of night. Anyways, as we rounded to the dark corner I picked, we did hear something that sounded like a janitor pushing his trash cart, but we just continued.

When we were "safe", she unbuckled my belt and pulled down my pants and proceeded to blow me BBBJ right there in the dark open. I was so damn turned on, but then we heard what I think was the janitor coming closer, so instead of risking getting caught we moved to another dark crevice, which wasn't hard to find. I picked this one again after she wanted to go to an area she knew, but I was still paranoid about her having her homies waiting for me, so I insisted and she didn't protest.

I did have a good amount to drink, but I wasn't so messed up that I wouldn't notice that she was ugly…again she wasn't bad looking at all for a middle-aged woman that I'm pretty sure was a deportee, plus she didn't smell.

So there we were, just me and her in some dark crevice near the Chaparral border. I was so turned on. I hadn't felt this type of horniness since junior high, so I couldn't help but let go.

She took control sucking me slow as she pulled down my pants, but I didn't let her pull them all the way down. She was giving me a slow BBBJ, and all I could hear was her sucking/smacking noise echo in the cool dark corner we were in.

I was so hypnotized with what was going on that I couldn't believe I was doing this in the open, and it felt so good, but then she stopped all of the sudden, and said that the cops were coming, and I should go that way while she went this way. I was so confused, so I did what she said as I pulled up my pants, but my senses started to come back and realized that she had stolen my phone. I wasn't going to chase her and make a scene… besides, I haven't experienced something like that at all in my life, so I just walked to a friend's house in San Ysidro and cancelled my phone. Yes, I walked at night in San Ysidro.

Well, she definitely knew how to give a BJ, and I probably would have taken her to a hotel if I had the money.

Amigo Commentary

Fotofreak: Damn son! At least you got a killer experience out of it… and hey! The new iPhone is out so you were probably planning on dropping a grand on a new phone anyway, right?

DonPisto: Well, look at it this way: you had an awesome experience, plus she didn't take your wallet, and you did not get mugged, thrown in the clink for public nudity, etc. I don't know anything about your cell phone, but it seems like you still came out ahead!

Fusion: Truth! It wasn't a special phone at all so I don't feel bad. I lose phones, so I usually get phones that aren't expensive. I still had everything that mattered on me, and looking back, the experience was almost priceless. I can still smell her shampoo on my hand 'cause I was resting it on her head as she blew me. At least she was clean. I won't be forgetting her name for a while: Erika.

Ivanho: Reminds me of the joke where the guy gets approached by a beautiful woman who gives him sex then steals his wallet. He goes out and buys some new wallets and keeps an empty one in his pocket and goes looking for her again. I think I will pull one of my old broken phones out of the drawer, stick it in my pocket, leave all my valuables in the hotel, and go look for her.

AmosRolling: This is a great, albeit extreme, example of the little head asserting the control and taking what most would consider an unacceptable risk.

SawGunner: I can see it now… an influx of gringos standing around in that area with broken cell phones in their pockets!

TomJackin: Can we get a map of the dark spots?

RussianPilot: OMG Fusion. First, thank you for your total honesty.

Secondly, you constantly refer to your cogency while admitting your state of inebriation. That should have been a screaming red flag in itself that your state of mind was not as aware and logical as you perceived.

Thirdly, your instinct. Dude, you're a veteran. To leave with less than $4 is absurd and to think for one second that a deportee wants your company for free? I'm just shocked because you know better.

When it sounds too good to be true, it always is.

FotoFreak: I'll disagree and I'd say he got a good deal out of it… an unusual experience involving a blowjob! Sure, he lost his phone but if it was a burner, then no big deal.

Fusion: Yeah, now that I've had some sleep, I'm actually kind of bummed out about it and now I'm worried about catching something. I do regret not keeping track of my money, but it happens to the best of us, and in these last few trips I've been doing what my buddy does and leaving my debit card at home so I couldn't take anything out. My phone is insured, so hopefully I can just look back on this as a pretty cool experience, one that I don't recommend doing though.

Mongers that might want the Fusion Experience Package will have to put themselves in a very risky spot at the 7-11 across the street from Hotel Nelson and at the very lonely hours of around 1-2am. She could be a walker, but I don't know. She could have been looking for a room, too, because the nights are getting colder, and I remember one very cold night when I used to walk to the border a lot, a lady selling flowers on the street begged me to take her to a room where she promised to blow me and fuck, too, after giving her a few dollars. I felt bad turning her down because it was freezing, but I couldn't get a room at that time.

In summary, well, whatever. It happened and I guess I'd rather get a BJ than an arm around my neck to choke me out or sucker punched. I'm kind going up and down with how I feel about it, but for the most part I don't feel too bad. And I keep reminding myself that my phone is insured so that helps, too.

Maverick: Objectively, a person should not expect to get robbed while getting a BJ. However, objectively a girl walking the street in Tijuana at night offering BJs should expect to get paid for her service, not burned when the deed is done.

In my book, the crime is allowing the service with no money to compensate her for it. Consider if she was honest and didn't rip you off—I would love to have seen the look on her face when you said, "But you said the only thing you wanted was my dick, and I took it literally!"

Fusion: All the girls say I'm "muy guapo" though! What can I say? My golden rod was doing all of the thinking. I think she took my phone because she wanted to tell her friends how great it was for her, so it's cool. Just kidding, of course.

I did tell her that I had no money, but she clung on to me to the point that I would have had to push her off while she was rubbing my dick and telling me that she wanted to blow me, but I didn't want to do that to her because that probably wouldn't have gone well. I did tell her that I didn't want to, and kept looking over my shoulder thinking someone was behind me waiting to jump me, but telling her okay finally got her off of me. I did think about running off when she let go, but I gave in to my curiosity and thought, "Fuck it. Let's see what happens," after she kept agreeing to my spots so easily.

Got my phone replaced, it was insured, and the old one was a little dinged up anyways. I checked to see if she made any calls, and no she didn't. It looks like she just saw some YouTube videos before I cancelled the line.

Moving forward, I hope not to do something like this again, and actually the alcohol has been affecting me differently lately, so I do want to start cutting back. I am a little paranoid about going back to Tijuana only to find out something was reported to the authorities, but I don't see how that would benefit her, and I don't know how they can make that connection now; so it's just me being paranoid and sober. I do plan to deny and ignore any walker that says they know me though.

It's not something I'm very proud of, but damn! I didn't think I had it in me!

Trip Trilogy

TJ500

New to the board. My handle is short for Tijuana 500, an homage to the Indy 500 or Daytona 500. I came up with the handle because I did so many laps on my first trip to Zona checking out the different bars and street girls.

I've lurked as a guest here and other boards and got enough info to make the initial journey safely, but being new and with my lack of Spanish, I still hit speed bumps as you will see.

This report is from three different trips that happened over the past three weeks.

Trip 1
Thursday in October

After doing the Tijuana 500, I ended up in Adelita. Filled the tank with beers and took in the place. I eventually approached a girl named Paula from Guadalajara. A blonde that stands in the area called Hottie Central. She is the ultimate shark, as you will find out.

I asked how much for an hour and she said $200. You guys are going to kill me, but I wasn't in the mood to haggle. I felt if you haggled it would provoke a weaker session. I forget who wrote if a girl doesn't hold your hand on the way up it's a bad sign. Well, as soon as I said yes, she was racing upstairs and I had trouble keeping up with her. Got upstairs and paid the $22. Again, she's racing to the room and I finally catch up. She asked for the money up front. Some say that's a bad sign but I didn't mind, but now I do. Anyway, we get down to business.

The BJ was okay and she never made eye contact. We make our way to mish and here is where it starts to go downhill. She puts her hand to block me from going all the way in and it's very awkward and uncomfortable for me. I can't speak Spanish and try to move her hand but she is saying something in Spanish. I asked to do doggy and I eventually finish in mish but everything just felt wrong. I don't expect these girls to really get into it but I've had more fun watching porn.

Anyway, we have an hour so I clean up and lay down to catch my second wind and chitchat to break the ice, hoping that would help the second session. Now get this… this is where it really goes off the deep end. She gets the other condom out and starts trying to get me up again with another CBJ. I'm not over the hill but I need a little break before the second round. I keep saying, "I need time," "Rest, please," "Ten or fifteen minutes." So she stops for maybe like a minute, while my hands are exploring I tried to suck on her breasts but she wouldn't let me. I never tried to kiss her but I doubt she would let me do that. Just a bored look on her faced and we are trying to talk but my lack of Spanish is taking us nowhere. She hears a song from downstairs and asked me the next time I come to buy her that CD. *What? Are you kidding me?* I say to myself. *Who does she think she is?*

But of course I say yes and she actually smiles and then back to silence. So after literally another minute passes, she's at it again trying to get me up and again I'm saying "I need time." So at this point she's looking at me like something is wrong with me and saying like she can't wait for me. More words are exchanged but the whole mood is taking a nose dive and I'm more mad than horny.

And then it comes to me, really it just boils down to one thing she wants to get in, get out, and get back downstairs as soon as possible. There is money to be made and I'm wasting her time.

I finally realize that and just say no more, "no mas" in my limited Spanish. Here is where I wish I didn't pay her up front. Because we were only in the room for a half and hour at that point and I only went once. So I go to clean up at the sink, and she is getting dressed and doing her makeup. Before I'm done, she is out the door. Whatever, welcome to TJ. I'm not rich but I can't get hung up on money. I probably should have complained but where would that have really gotten me? That is what this board is for.

So I make my way back down to the bar and think about picking up another girl. While I'm sitting there, this guy asks me how did it go. I tell him and he said he could tell by the look on my face. He says don't worry about it. He said he has been there and done that and says no more.

I asked him if repeating with her helps and he said no. She starts asking for gifts, CDs, candy, etc. And the sessions don't get any better, only worse if you don't bring something. He says not that she gets jealous really but she doesn't like it if you go up with other girls. I don't get that. These girls go up with a ton of guys; how can they be jealous? He just says it's because it's money out of her pocket. He went up with another girl one time and went with her next and she way under-performed to sort of punish him. I asked him about the hand at the "Y" move and he said just grab her wrist and move it. Not sure if this guy posts here but he should remember me by this story. He was a big help. But that's enough about Paula until Trip III…

Trip II
The Following Tuesday

Decided to hang in Chicago Club this time. I like this place. Everyone says the girls are hotter in AB but I found these girls to be just as hot but with better attitudes.

I met this very beautiful girl named Sonya from Sinaloa. She is a petite brunette. I can't get over how pretty her face is. I ask her how much for an hour and she says $140. Probably still too high for the veterans, but this is $60 less than Paula and she is just as hot. Sonya has small breasts but great legs. When she is naked, you can tell she had a baby by the stomach stretch marks but everything else is great. CBJ with eye contact. I like that very much and from there on, the first session went as expected. We tried to talk during the break. The Spanish and English was limited, but it was fun trying to communicate rather than a bore. The second session was awesome, too. She took a good time in the shower so she gets an A in cleanliness. Worth everything I paid. She sits in the left alcove when you enter.

Trip III
Thursday in November

I decided to go to AB again. I sat down at the bar on the right when you enter. So I'm sitting there and these two blondes come up to me. They say, "You went with Paula before." (I guess she pointed me out to them on Trip I, "See that stupid white guy with the unhappy look on his face? He's easy money.") They tell me that they are her sisters. Their names are Eilene and Myra. Eilene says "Buy us a drink." I say no thank you.

Now mind you, my back is leaning against the bar and they are facing me so they can see the bartender. All of a sudden, two of those small beers appear in their hands and the bartender is asking me for $14. I guess she ordered them in Spanish while I was talking to Myra. The place is loud and I'm trying to say I didn't order them, I turn to the girls who are smiling and I eat it again. $14 and tip down the drain.

Now here is what really pisses me off: after they get those drink tickets, they walk away and throw their beers away in that big gray trash can at the bar. They took maybe three sips. I wish I had grabbed the tickets before they did, but options are clear hindsight. Well, anyway, I finish my beer and head to CC. I never saw Paula. I guess she was upstairs. But I wasn't there to see her anyway, hoping to find someone else. However, after that scam I had to get out.

I tried to find Sonya but no luck. But found another hottie that hangs in the alcove. Her name is Deanira or something like that. I think I got it wrong though because I've never heard a name like that before. She is from Sonora. Her hair is strawberry blonde or some form of blonde. Has a navel piercing that is sexy. I ask her how much for one hour and she says $120. The price just keeps on dropping with no effort. She speaks perfect English so we had no problems communicating whatsoever. The two sessions where awesome and she showered after each. A+ on cleanliness. I highly recommend this girl, too.

My AB experience may be an exception to the norm. I don't care. I just know what to avoid now and look out for. Maybe I'm just a repugnant looking white guy and had newbie written all over me, but Sonya and Deanira treated me very well. Can't wait to see them again!

Fast Times on a Wild Wednesday Night

EL OSO

El Oso went to the Zona on Wednesday night!! There were quite a few extra chicas working as compared to previous Wednesdays!! I saw a chica at Cuartos Teresa, wearing a gold sequin bra and open stomach showing!! I felt the urge to check her out more closely!! I saw it was the novia of Sonero [IQ 165]!! Yet I decided to talk with her anyway!!

She told me her name is Veeney or so it sounded!! Not certain about the correct spelling, but more important she had BIG BOOBS and a very cute face; with a welcoming smile!!

I asked her what it would cost for the great time in the room in pesos and she said, "200 pesos y 50 for ze room"!! So we went inside and she was very sweet and cute 20 or 21; just slightly chubby, yet she had BIG TITS!! So I boned her for about 19 minutes and finally the knock came on the door; so we got up and I gave her 200p plus a 14.5 peso teep!! She has a really a great personality, yet only average in terms of performance!!

I went back outside, and went to Tomjackin's stand and had a few tacos de birria!! Then I continued to get some good exercise just walking up and down the streets!! All the people I saw in the Zona Norte were good Catholics who were very honorable in every aspect of life!!

Then I walked past Ysabel at La Ribera and she was wearing these super sexy LONG false eyelashes that just made me jump around and go right up to her with great zest!! Never before has she looked soooo SEXY!! So we went to the office and I gave the guy 70 pesos; and we headed upstairs to ze cuarto!! We got inside, took off our clothing, and she slapped the condom on my super screaming erection!! I got on top in missionary, and she was really moving around, bumping and grinding just like a bucking Bronco would do!! Of course I have never tried doing it with a bucking Bronco, but I can just use my imagination on that account!!

She was really doing it with me like her life depended on it, and I came with a great screaming orgasm after only about 4 minutes and 29 seconds!! But it sure was great while it lasted!! I gave her 200p and while I was reaching for extra money to geeve her a teep she just shot out the door; and went down the stairs!! Maybe she has an aversion to Bears; yet she was SUPERSONIC FANTASTICO for the time we were on the bed together!!

Then about 20 minutes later, I saw HereAndThere [IQ168] and he is a super nice guy who spends lots of time in the library studying all sorts of subjects!! He is very thoughtful of others and is always looking out for others before himself!! A very unusual and special quality to find nowadays!! So we walked and talked for about 50 minutes; and then he went to El Porton to do some studying of advanced Computer Engineering!!

At 10:55pm, I caught the ruta back to the border, and I was called up by a guy named ALVAREZ and he just said to me "Go ahead," without even checking my passport!! I guess I look like a very mellow Bear who would never cause problems!!

Then when I was walking in SAN YSIDRO, a really trashy looking bum came to me and said "Ehhh, I geeve jew a ride to Los Angeles."

I said, "No thanks!!"

Then he said, "Okay. I geeve jew a ride to San Diego."

I said, "No thanks!!"

Then he said, "Jew got 50 cents for me, bro?"

And I just said, "Nope!! I am meeting my wife just three blocks north of here!!" Then he went the other way!!

HOPE TO HAVE AT LEAST 998,993 MORE GREAT TIMES IN THE ZONA NORTE DE TIJUANA!!!

An Evil Force Overtook Me

CATFISH

Last Saturday, an evil force took control of my car and steered me south when I should have been heading north, challenging my monger virgin fears. I drove across about noon or so, cruising down Constitución steeling my nerves. I forgot my handy little map so I parked at the high-priced lot on Revo and went for a walk. I decided Adelita would be the easiest place to pop my TJ cherry. I was just as lost on foot but eventually found my way. Once through the door, I had to laugh at my initial fear of walking there. Maybe it wasn't so much fear as shame. Piece of cake. I can't remember who wrote it but another monger said he walks everywhere with a sense of urgency and people leave him alone. Great advice. My crutch was my cell phone. They tend to bother you less if you appear busy.

Thanks to all you mongers out there and this site for making my first trip as easy as ordering French toast at Denny's. I walked straight to the bar, ordered a beer, and looked around the place. It seemed as familiar as my own living room.

The first chick that caught my eye was standing near the first set of booths near Hottie Central on the way to the baño. Fairly petite, nice white top showing off decent B cups. Some guy obviously recovering from middle-age crisis snatched her up. When they came back, I got a closer look at her and she had this look on her face like she just took a healthy bite of dog shit. Talk about a bad vibe. Pass.

Some older lady wearing a loose blouse rushed into the place and hurriedly fondled each of us at the bar. No thanks! I was only approached about three or four times in the hour it took for me to decide to finally go up, which was nice because I wanted to soak in the "real" club fantasy.

Finally settled on Anna-Marie from Mexico for sixty. I had turned down younger, cuter advances, but I had just the right amount of beer in me by now and she promised to please. Appearance was not nearly as big a factor as attitude on this first trip.

Up in the room; money up front. Whatever. Stripped down and got a nice massage. The hilarity of her fake papayas rubbing across my ass and my shit-eatin' grin in the mirror struck me as funny so it took a little work to get the condom on. Great CBJ then on to our first position, which I don't know if there's a name for it. Kind of like a reverse cowgirl but with my legs around her. GREAT view. Changed to mish where I finished selfishly fast. Got my rocks and today that's all that mattered. Gotta get through kindergarten somehow. Tipped her a couple bucks then headed down for more.

Downed another beer and headed for the john. On my way in and on my way out, this timid little creature caught my eye. I went back to the bar for another round checking out the scene, but carefully watching timid one. Dog-shit Face was heading up for her third or fourth poke. I was tempted with the mileage she was getting this early in the afternoon. There must be something about her…

Finally, I got the timid Juanita de Veracruz to sit with me. She did not speak a lick of English. Uh-oh, time to put on the Spanish thinking cap. No kids, no family in TJ, just workin' to get back home. Bought her one Coke and talked until my Spanish was exhausted. She was bored off her ass, twirling her hair, which oddly was working for me. After refusing a couple more fichas, she brought up el cuarto. We settled on fifty.

Up in the room, she was even more shy. I never knew this would be such a turn on. Even the bra was slow to come off. Only then did I learn she was just 18. I had to do the translation in my head a couple times. "Did she just say 18?" Lovely smooth perky breasts with neat small nipples. Not a single flaw. Stuck with straight mish musing at her clumsy pelvic thrusts. Paid her for her time after a quick shower solo and off she went. Hit the pavement and kept walking as I was already five hours late.

For some this may seem like a hurried waste of time with all TJ has to offer, but for me, a recent AMP monger, for the price of one FS in SD, I got to pretend I got lucky with not one but two chicks in a club! Another fantasy fulfilled.

Another First Timer's Report

Georgie Orgie

I was in San Diego last week on business and couldn't help trying out some of the tips and techniques I learned from in here. Then why, oh why, do I not follow the advice given? Anyway, it was an interesting experience. Here's the brief version:

Went to TJ at about 2pm by taking the trolley from San Diego to Tijuana. It took about an hour, but there is a convenient drop-off right at the border. Hopped in a cab to Revo; five bucks with tip. I wanted to walk around Revo a little bit first, just to get my bearings and ease into the scene. I never got hassled any more than the typical "Hey Amigo, blah blah blah." Went into the stores and took in some of the local flea market scene.

I hit two bars on Revo. The first was El Tigre. By myself, I immediately doubled the customer count in the place (and I think the other guy was a boyfriend of one of the dancers). They had one long stage in the small interior. A hottie dancer was getting a dance lesson from another girl. Dull.

Almost immediately, I was approached by a chica who was sitting with about four other chicas who were all looking bored out of their minds. The chica who approached me was introduced by a hostess, but I politely said I wanted to just watch for awhile. The chica sat back down in line. After finishing my beer ($3), I left.

Next stop: Animals (I think. I may be completely wrong about the name though). I don't remember seeing much posted about this place. It has a much larger interior than the other clubs and has private booths upstairs for lappers. This time, there were three other patrons in the place, and only about three girls. The one that was introduced to me was unattractive (which explains why she wasn't sitting with anyone.) The waiter came over and I ordered a Corona ($4). I gave him a fiver and he immediately pulled the old switcheroo, showing me a single and repeating, "Señor, the beer is $4."

Good God man, for a stinking five? Give me a break. I firmly insisted I gave him a five, and he eventually brought my beer.

There was one absolutely smoking chica in the place. She was a blonde, and was wearing a tight white two-piece outfit. She was sitting with an older guy and didn't leave him until she got up to dance. She gave a decent dance, and a $1 tip in her panties got me a nice feel of her shaved pussy and a kiss. I wanted to get a lap dance from her after her set, but she went to the booth with the older guy, and I didn't want to hang around and wait, plus the next dancer was not very good looking.

So on to Adelita. I took a cab from Revo over there ($4). Probably a rip, but I didn't have my handy map and didn't feel like walking. When I got there, I went right into AB. By now, it was about 3:30pm on a weekday. Inside, the only action was around the main stage. There were TONS of chicas in the place, and slightly fewer guys than that. Enough that you never felt conspicuous, but not too many that you had to vie for attention from the ladies.

I headed right back to Hottie Central, but nothing was going on. The women back there were the same as the rest of the women. All of them hit just about every range: from lowly 3s to stunning 8s and 9s. I got groped a couple of times by a few average chicas, but didn't want to get tied down just yet. I wanted to look around some more. I made a lap around the bar and took it all in. The tables around the main stage were all full, with some pretty serious hands-on dancing and tipping going on with the dancing chica. I would say I got approached by about five different chicas in the first 15 minutes there, but I wasn't really interested in any of them.

I hit the head a couple of times, too, to lose the beers I had been consuming. The men's room was okay, but I was a little peeved at the attendants. The first time in there, I got a single paper towel from the guy after standing there for a few moments with wet hands. I gave him a buck, as advised. The second time I went in there, I was about to stiff him, because he was talking to another attendant and not paying attention to the patrons. I got a throat clear from the guy as he pointed to his empty tip box. Whatever. Enough of that.

I went back out to the floor and walked up to this absolutely gorgeous petite young thing. She was standing and talking to another chica. She had a tight white dress on. Dark hair, small chest, very cute. I asked her if I could buy her a drink in a secluded booth. She looked at me blankly as her friend said she didn't speak English. Great. That made two of us. I had the friend interpret my intentions (or at least some of them) and she agreed to have a drink. We went to the far back booth past the stage on the right and had a drink. She was willing to cuddle with me in the booth, and she was grabbing me outside my pants, but she seemed extremely shy. I got out of her that she was 18. I'd definitely believe it.

Despite not knowing much English, she knew enough to point to "upstairs" with her finger and to quote me "$60" for "sucky and fucky."

I tried to negotiate "just sucky" with her, to no avail. She said she knew what I was talking about, but said it was still $60 for sucky and fucky. She also pointed to her butt and said "no." I was really only after a BJ, so $60 seemed a bit steep for that, especially with someone that I could not communicate or negotiate with. So reluctantly, I let her get away.

A little later, I approached another hot chica. I would rate her about an 8. She was a bit of a Cleveland Brown though… you know, great uniform, bad helmet. She gets a 9 for body—petite, slim, very tight ass, smooth legs, small chest, and tight stomach. She gets a 6 for face, though. But hey, I wasn't going to be kissing her, right? Besides, her ass and legs were just way too good to pass up.

So we sat down for a drink and were soon joined by a friend of hers. And here is when I started deviating from the advice from all of my brothers in this site. She began talking to her friend while we were having a drink. She let me rub her back, legs, head, whatever. I stuck my hand down the back of her cute blue plaid skirt and rubbed her ass, all while she showed little interest. I asked about a dance, and she said she didn't dance. She did say, though, that I could take her upstairs from $50. Then, she went back to talking. To her credit, the friend at least struck up a bit of a conversation with me, but not much of interest.

It was getting late, and I decided I might as well just go for it. I asked the hottie if she would take $40, and she said yes. So we went upstairs. Her name was Marinda.

So what is the advice I failed to listen to so far? Those that don't mess around much downstairs aren't going to be very interesting upstairs. And boy, was that true.

She led me upstairs (she walked in front while I tried to keep up). When we got up into the room, she went right into her purse and pulled out a condom and lube. She turned to look at me and told me to take my clothes off, and then she turned around and took hers off. She then got onto the bed and laid there on her back with her arms out. I got on top of her and began kissing her neck. She laid there. I kissed her breasts. She laid there. I fingered her, and she reached for the condom. She put that on quickly and put her legs up, but I wasn't going there yet. I got up on her chest and she took me into her mouth.

Not to spoil the story, but this was the only good part. She was pretty decent at this, and she allowed me to hold her head and really direct the action. But soon she kind of pushed me away and reached for the lube. Unfortunately, I didn't protest and allowed this to happen. She then grabbed me and directed me into her. I was a little weak-kneed to protest at this point. After a bit of very uninteresting pumping, she asked if I wanted doggie style. We did that for a bit and I came. She let me stay inside her for a little bit, until I pulled out. When I did, she got up and immediately went into the shower. I took the condom off and got in with her. She never faced me in the shower—just let me grab her from behind while she washed. She finished quickly and got out, leaving me to finish on my own.

By the time I got out, she was almost dressed and we still had about 10 minutes left (yeah, I know, but did I mention she had an extremely hot body?). I tried to rub her a little bit more, but she kind of shied away. Once I got dressed, she opened the door and was gone. I practically had to chase her to the front desk.

Oh, by the way, I tipped the towel guy a buck. He was talking to another guy in the hallway and said, "Hey, how about for my guy here?" Whatever. I followed Marinda downstairs and outside, then hopped into a cab without even going back into the club.

So all in all, not a great experience—about a 4, only because I was grabbing an awesome ass while I came.

AMIGO COMMENTARY

EL FANATICO: The good news is that if you continue going to TJ, this will probably be your worst trip. We've all had trips like this, where nothing goes quite right. I can tell you did your homework and handled things pretty well though. Once you find a favorita or two that never fail to deliver GFE, you'll be positive that TJ is the promised land.

The only suggestion I have is that if a chica does that sprint ahead of you thing as you're walking up with her, let her go.

When she comes back, just make up some excuse such as that you can't find your cash.

COLDCRUSH: Never go up with a girl who doesn't hold your hand when she takes you upstairs. If she walks ahead of you, it's like she's telling the whole bar you aren't shit.

Don't feel bad. My first TJ fuck was bullshit also. I took up some chica named Isabel at Chicago Club. Nice, big fat ass like I like, tig ol' bitties, good oral skills (though it was with a freaking rubber), but the girl wouldn't kiss. Luckily, later on I found a freaking hottie dancing at HK who took me up for $50, and stayed with me like an hour and a half. Unfortunately, I was drunk off my ass by then, and I don't even know if I asked her what her name was, much less remember what it was. I guess someone fell asleep at Cascadas or something that night, because there was never a knock and she stayed with me until the sun came up… and right before I took her up, I got hit on by a hottie who I took up the next time, who became an instant fav.

MADDOG: Great job. You would have been more disappointed in her performance if she had sucked $60 out of you. Live and learn.

First Trip to Adelita

EPITHUMIA

After going to Tijuana for many years and hitting Revolución for all its worth, I have discovered Zona Norte thanks to fellow mongers.

Day started at noon with 100mg of Viagra and a fatty joint before the border. After crossing, I had a bucket of beer and four shots of tequila. Great start!

Checked out Revolución searching for my young diamond in the rough. In the Unicorno, I was molested by lesbian looking girls trying to give me a blowjob. As they stroked my dick, I had to remind myself that it is only the liquor trying to persuade me to partake. Shooed them off. A real hottie was dancing next and I kept her on the maybe list. Checked out Peanuts & Beer and found it is now only Peanuts club. It's also upstairs. It also sucked. More lesbians stroking the old johnson, trying to hawk girls for $80 for everything. I ask what was everything and found it was everything... minus sex. One said she didn't have her health card. It made me wonder if girls who can't get their health card go and work Revolución.

At this point, I decide to take 20mg of Cialis on top of 100mg of Viagra I already had in my system. Got my picture on the Mexican zebra and continued hunting.

Now, on to Adelita!

Man, I was a true kid in the candy store. The problem isn't finding a hottie, it's deciding whom. It was only 4pm. After checking out the wares, I decided on a hot little number named Vanessa. She was 24 with streaked blonde hair and hairless everywhere else. Got a session for $60 (sorry guys, but I was VERY drunk by now and not in the mood to negotiate). Got in the room and got naked. She gave me a decent blowjob for a few minutes. She then insisted on doggie. Works for me, but she was kind of a mood killer with "Oh duele!" and "Mas despacio!"

I only had 20 minutes to finish and wanted to get off. I wasn't going to get off with slow sex. Well, after a few I was tired and frustrated with her slowing me down so I got on my back and took off my condom for a handjob to finish me off. She got frustrated with my endurance and so did I. I finally finished a little over time, but never got "the knock." I asked to take her picture but she didn't seem to like the idea. I offered her $5 but she still refused. Oh well. No tip for her.

Looks: 8.5

Attitude: 4

Experience: 6 (I'm being generous because she was really hot!)

Checked out the street girl scene. Pretty gross, guys. Saw two that were acceptable, but didn't partake. Chicago was dead. Tropical seemed like a locals club that had more ranchero dancing than sex. Girls were a little too thick for me. Went back to Adelita and I sat around buying ficha drinks and talking to the girls. One girl said they have to sell ten drinks a night and another said twenty. Who's right?

They all seem pretty aware of the internet and fear family seeing them in pictures. A lot don't seem to really like TJ or the scene, but hey it's a living. One girl said $800 for toda la noche. Everything but the culo, she said. She advised finding the girls over 30 or that seemed lonely or fat to proposition for the culo. BBBJ is reasonably common, but most girls won't admit to it in the bar according to one.

I felt very safe everywhere in TJ because there were two of us and it was daytime. As we drunkenly went pharmacy to pharmacy, we found we weren't on Revolución and were on Constitución. Glad I remembered the map!

Went by all the map designated "danger zones" and realized that I was bigger than 90% of the locals; it was the visitors from LA that made me nervous (gang bangers). The locals were kind of annoying though. "Hey meeester, want a massage?", "Hey meester, want some coca?", "Hey meeester, want some panocha?", etc, etc.

Got the bacon-wrapped hot dogs and they were awesome. I decided that a hot dog with a ham center and bacon wrapping would be the ultimate pig dog. Tacos were good; hope it was cow and not cat!

Ended the trip by smuggling a vial of generic Stadol across the border. The vet has the best meds after all.

Plan on going straight to Adelita next time and drinking less. I will get some two-on-one action and a BBBJ.

Overall, a great trip. As I came across the border I was asked, "Are you bringing anything back from Mexico?" I replied, "I hope not! My girlfriend would kill me."

BTW, I am still getting a hard-on every hour with no external stimuli. It's been well over 24 hours since I took the Cialis and Viagra mix. I suspect it's the Cialis causing the reaction because Viagra never did this before.

I Can't Remember Her Name

Zepequeno

It's something like Filomena, but I don't think that's it. She's got sort of an Asian-ish face. Long dark hair, with some blonde streaks. Small tits with decent nipples. No waist to speak of. Very aggressive. I've seen her only on the upper part of the main floor, next to the stage. On Wednesday, she grinded me on the floor for a dollar. It was quite nice, and I needed a rev-up for my second session with another girl, so I took her to the privado area for $20. That was good also. She tried to get me to go to the hotel, but she wasn't my type, so I declined. I just wanted a bit of rubbing to be sure I was ready to have Round 2 with someone else…

So on Thursday, I went the same route. Using her for a bit of post-session/pre-next-session stimulation. Did the dollar grind for a while, and then bought her a drink, hoping for some manual stim in the booth. She then told me about the VIP room. She got the waiter to explain it was $80 for ten beers and the room. And any other price for the girl would be negotiated separately. The girl said she wanted to go, and that no propina would be necessary. I thought she wanted to go because she was very horny—as the day before—and because she was getting enough of the cut of the $80. So how bad could it be, right? I told her I wanted sucky sin condom, and she said yes to that and everything else. Todo. So okay. Let's go!

We get up there and the room looks down on the second floor balcony. Waiter brings the bucket of beer. She begins drinking while sitting on my lap. Things began rather slowly, as she was quite interested in the beer. But as before, she was really horny. She's kind of a nympho. But she's also kind of an alcoholic. The first night, I declined also because she seemed drunk, like sloppy drunk. Slurred speech drunk. And on this Thursday, she confirmed my assessment.

She went like a house on fire—every position…impossible positions… but the BBBJ was horrendous. I had to remind her several times, and loudly, that she agreed to it, and she finally responded with a couple of snake licks and nothing else. I had to take the condom from her so she wouldn't keep trying to put it on…

Eventually, I got tired of that battle so we start banging, and to be honest, the lap dances were better, even though she really did hump me like it was her last day on earth. The problem wasn't the effort. It was that she was so uninterested in what I was feeling and completely interested in her own orgasm/s. Which is fine, if she's a civilian, but not so much if I'm paying.

We were at it for an hour, and it was all quite sweaty. But her lack of attentiveness, and me constantly trying to get her to understand the word STOP made it impossible for me to finish. I then asked her to use her hand, and she started stroking me as if she'd never given a hand job before. Her knuckle or something was digging into me, so I had to stop that as well. I had to finish myself, with her rubbing one out on herself, and her directing me to shoot onto her clit. That might sound good, but it wasn't.

That might have all been fine, but as we're getting dressed, I thought I would reward her for the effort… not for the results. Now remember, she originally said no tip/compensation. I handed her a 200-peso note. She pulled out her phone to use as a light to inspect the bill. Then she said, "No. Two more like this."

She wanted 600! I reminded her she said that no tip was necessary. I never would have gone to VIP with her if the price was going to be more than $80. I could have gone to the hotel with someone I was really attracted to for $85 total. With a better room and a shower. I went to VIP with her because I wanted to see the VIP with the one-way glass thing as I got a sloppy BBBJ.

Finally, I ended up giving her another 200 pesos. And she still wanted another 200. I said no.

And she drank all ten beers in that hour. ALL. TEN.

HK Chica Has a Real Talent

DR. F

I realized that I forgot to pack my cologne as I was approaching the border so I decided to stop at the outlet mall at San Ysidro for lunch. I did a little shopping, and while I was browsing at Ralph Lauren, I noticed they had numerous cologne testers at the front of the store. Back in high school (circa 1984/1985), I used to wear Polo cologne as almost all my friends did, so I was getting a little nostalgic for those days. If you remember, back in the 80s, there weren't the hundreds of colognes to choose from like there are now. There were about five for older men (Old Spice, Aqua Velva, Kanon, Grey Flannel) and not many more for younger men (Polo, Drakkar Noir, Aramis, Azzaro). But now there are so many fragrances that even Ralph Lauren has about a half-dozen choices for men.

So instead of spritzing on the old green Polo like I did hundreds of times in my youth, I reached for one called Polo Black and covered my neck in a fine mist. The chicas were bound to enjoy me a little more now!! It was a new scent for me, as I currently prefer Bulgari, Acqua di Gio, or Lacoste White.

From there, I parked my car and walked across and caught a taxi to HK/Cascadas, where I was staying for one night. I dropped my bag in the room and headed downstairs.

I ran into Jazz inside HK. I'd been with her before. My very first experience with her was super hot (in the booth), then super cold and disastrous in the room. Well, because I find her so cute and our chemistry in the booth so off-leash, I rekindled our mini romance and bedded her again with much better results.

Anyway, aside from our absolutely fantastic sexual energy in the booth over the course of two fichas, what really blew my mind about this chica was the following conversation in half-ass Spanish:

> Me: *(nuzzling her neck)* I like your scent. *(I didn't particularly, but I was flirting and practicing a new phrase at the same time!)*
>
> Her: Thanks. Let me smell you. *(She does as I fondle her tits.)* Hey, I like that. What fragrance is it?
>
> Me: If you guess correctly, I'll buy you another ficha.
>
> Her: Okay, let me think. It smells familiar.
>
> Me: *(sarcastic tone)* Yeah, good luck.

I thought there was no way this chica could guess my scent from the hundreds out there for men, particularly Polo Black, which is relatively new and probably not worn by many Mexicanos.

> Her: *(after a few minutes of really exercising her brain)* My guess is Polo Black.
>
> Me: *(flabbergasted and in English)* Are you fucking kidding me?!

We just laughed like hyenas and I ordered the second ficha—as I was planning on doing all along—but she was absolutely beaming for the rest of our time together.

In summary: although Jazz can't really fuck (I wouldn't recommend her in the room), she's a great little flirt and a total savant when it comes to distinguishing men's cologne. Quite a talent, I must admit.

Amigo Commentary

DickArmy: I've heard of Cheap Charlies before and I might have been called one a couple times. But that's an Advanced Cheap Charlie move to get your scent on at the sample counter in the mall. You might be the OG of Cheap Charlies. I wonder if they have a knock off version of Polo Black at the 99.

PapaJones: How could you leave BRUT off that list? Still wear it (by the way) and the chicas go FUCKING WILD over it!

TomJackin: I'm too old and cheap to smell good. So I just rub my body with 200-peso notes… the girls go fucking wild!

Rancheroi: Chicas in the zone often will give me a sniff to smell the fragrance that I am wearing, and they correctly guess the fragrance is a thick wad of 50, 100, and 200 peso bills in my pocket. It always makes their nipples stiffen up a bit and they get this big smile on their faces when that smell hits their nose.

Matiz: In addition to the colognes (*ahem,* "aftershaves"; real men don't use cologne) you mentioned, were perennial "old guy" favorites like Jai Karate, Canoe, Brut (hawked by Joe Namath), and my personal favorite in high school, English Leather. Every now and again, I'll catch a whiff of that distinctive English Leather fragrance, usually emanating from some fossilized old geezer who's been applying it liberally like mosquito repellent since the Kennedy administration, and it will remind me of Debbie N., my very first date. Short skirts and slutty blonde looks, but a total prick tease. I only got LFK at the door, no second base, did not repeat. Perhaps if I'd had Polo Black, I would have gotten farther.

RyGuy and The Homeboys' First Trip to TJ

RyGuy

What's up guys! Man, I had my first trip to TJ and it was badass!! Me and homeboys left home at about three and rolled up there at about 7 o'clock with the shitty ass traffic. That was the only bad part about the trip, the drive down. But anyways, on to the good story of it.

Me and my three friends parked on the US side for 7 bucks and walked across. We immediately took a cab to the zone and headed straight to Adelita. Oh, one other thing… those cab drivers are crazy ass drivers, cutting in front of people and ripping the corners with the cheap ass wheels on those cabs barely hanging on; that was a little scary.

The zone was pretty shady with tons of people on the street that looked questionable but we went straight into the club and we all had some Bud Lights, enough to start feeling a little kicked back. There were so many people in that club, tons of Mexican hombres and Americans looking for some tail, and man, there was plenty of pussy to go around. There were so many hot chicas there that I didn't know who to go up with first. I told my friend that we should circle inside the bar and take a look at the prospects for the night.

We had tons of chicas coming up to us asking to suck 'n fuck but we kept turning 'em down for a while 'til we found the right ones. My first chick had her eyes staring hard on me for the first hour while we were drinking. (They all stare, but this one was doing it intently). I took a good look. She had black shoulder-length hair, C cups, nice DSL (dick sucking lips) and a hot ass. She was the first chick that I would take up.

I waited for her to come up to me and I had her for 40 bucks. Ha! Originally, she said $60, and I was in no way going to pay what they were asking, so she caved for not that much. But I just had her give me a blowjob 'cause I didn't want to screw her although she wasn't bad.

The next chick I had was AMAZING. I saw this woman and she was the tightest bodied woman I had seen around. Her name was Larrana. She had an extremely fit, toned body, round perfect bubbly ass, great legs, lips, and tits. You name it and she had it, as this perfect chica was amazing. She teabagged me, sucked me, and started riding on top of me. I hit her spread eagle, then doggy style, which was the best, might I add, with that tight ass. Even her pussy was tight!! Man, I hit her up like there was no tomorrow. She was moaning and screaming like crazy! If you get with any chick there, GO WITH Larrana. I had her for a 50 and it was worth every penny.

We had a great experience for our first trip. The last chick I hit had another great ass. I just have a thing with perfect round booties, and I'm sure you guys do, too. She was no Larrana but she still had awesome moves.

I made use of all of those half-hour sessions. My whole trip cost me like $220 with gasoline, food, tips , drinks, girls. I have never had so much fun for so little money!

I will tell you one more thing: I will never go to a strip club in California and pay that kind of money ever again! Thank you to everyone at TJAmigos for the great advice and for helping a group out for this first trip. We couldn't have done it without you.

Oh, and one more thing…I'm gonna learn how to speak Spanish fluently. I wanna know those things she was moaning. Thanks Amigos…

No One Here Gets Out Alive

KENDRICKS

Five to one, baby, one in five
No one here gets out alive, now
You get yours, baby, I'll get mine
Gonna make it, baby if we try

I was kicked back, just drinking a beer in the newly remodeled Peanuts & Beer and watching a fine ass Latina rip off her g-string, all to the tune of a new electro-grunge band reinterpreting The Doors classic.

Having just finished an hour-long fuckfest with a wonderfully skilled Adelita goddess, I intended only to have a couple of brews, watch some titties bouncing, and head out. But the vision on stage had hypnotized me, and I was slowly changing my plans.

Your ballroom days are over, baby
Night is drawing near
Shadows of the evening crawl across the years

She caught me staring at her and smiled. After slithering her way across the stage, she wrapped her arms around me, kissed me, and ran her hands across my chest and arms.

Ya walk across the floor with a flower in your hand
Trying to tell me no one understands
Trading your hours for a handful dimes
Gonna make it, baby, in our prime

I reached out to feel one of her magnificent tits, and she threw a leg over my shoulder, giving me access to that sweet little panocha, if only for a minute. Her hand wandered to my crotch before leaving, bringing my weary Lazarus back to life. Without a doubt, one of the best dollars I have ever spent.

Get together one more time
Get together, got to
Take you up in my room and…
Hah-hah-hah-hah-hah

I continued to sip my beer as I enjoyed the show. She had dark morena skin, wild hair, big bouncy tits, a small tight waist, and full swivel hips. I couldn't take my eyes off of her. I had to have her.

Love my girl
She lookin' good, lookin' real good
Love ya, c'mon

She collected her tips and clothes off the dance floor and stepped off the stage. I hurried to snag her for a lap dance, before anyone else got in my way.

"Twenty dollars lap dance two songs, sixty dollars blow job, eighty dollars, everything." One of the waitresses had already butted in, eager to make a tip.

"Just the lap dance. That's all I need."

The waitress hated me. I had already waved off three or four different girls she had brought by, and now I was turning down sex with a hottie. Disgust and loathing burned in her eyes, but I didn't care. I paid for the dance, tipped the waitress a buck, and headed for one of the private booths with my new friend.

Once in the booth, she immediately stripped down to her g-string, and asked if I wanted to fuck. Having just been put through an excruciatingly satisfying wringer in the Hotel Coahuila, I was momentarily content just to feel this hottie up for a couple of songs, and cross the border with a few dollars in my pocket for a change.

Content, that is, until she reached into my pants and fondled my balls while kissing my neck and tonguing my ear. My hands had free reign over her incredible hardbody while blood surged into my cock.

"Come on baby, twenty dollars more for blowjob."

An offer I couldn't refuse.

I pulled a twenty and a vanilla flavored condom out of my pocket and handed her both. She unrolled the rubber onto my throbbing hard-on, and hungrily bobbed and slurped while I played with her hot tits and ran my fingers through her hair.

Without saying a word, she stood up, took off her g-string, and lowered her pussy onto my shaft. The head of my cock parted her cunt lips, and she slowly impaled herself onto me.

I thrust up in my chair to meet the grinding of her hips as she brutally violated me. The pounding music pulsed through my head as I desperately held her close to me, burying my face between her tits as I drove deeply inside her hot little box.

This one wasn't going to last long. Every nerve in my body was on edge, and I completely surrendered my body to her merciless grind. There's nothing like burying the bone inside of a hot lapdancer in a club, minutes after she stepped off the stage.

If this is wrong, I don't want to be right.

My orgasm ripped through my body and brain as I bucked and

drove tightly against her. She smiled and kissed me, then ground out every last drop before rising away.

"Next time you come, we go to hotel together, okay, baby?" I nodded my agreement before putting my cock away. She kissed me again, and then led me back into the club.

No one here may get out alive, but as the man said,
I'm going to get my kicks before the whole shit house
goes up in flames…

THE FREAKIEST BARGIRL I EVER MET

SECRETAMIGOX

After some time to decompress I have decided to write a short report on Dilan, the freakiest BG, if not the freakiest girl period, I've ever fucked.

It was Sunday night, late October. I had a room in Cascadas and I was on the second night of my trip, so at that point I was just casually roaming HK, browsing at the available talent. A pair of chicas stopped me and asked if I wanted to arriba them for a threesome. The hard-selling mouth piece was kind of squat and didn't impress me, but her friend Dilan was tall, skinny, and looked like a young pre-boob job Francesca Le. I was so sick of seeing grotesque basketball fake asses and goldfish-eye looking botched boob jobs that her natural, tall, waifish look really hit the spot. I said I don't want a threesome but I did want to arriba her friend. A price was struck and the story begins...

Upstairs, Dilan spoke perfect English and was frisky from the get-go. Had I not pushed the envelope, she would already have been an ATF based on the GFE service alone. But then all hell broke loose when I saw a depraved look in her eyes during mish, and I decided to put my hands on her neck and started choking her in a firm but measured manner. Her eyes lit up and told me to go harder and be rough with her.

"You like it rough, huh?" and slapped her right across her face.

She said, "Thank you, sir."

I knew then that it was on.

From there, it was a blur of slapping, spanking, hair pulling, choking, fish-hooking, and deep throat gagging that would make Max Hardcore proud. The defining moment of the night was when we switched to doggy and I wrapped my arms around her neck and put her in a rear naked choke while I was fucking her. She kept asking me to go hard, so I tightened the choke. I let go of the chokehold after counting three Mississippis, and she dropped face first on the mattress like a sack of potatoes and was out like a light. I immediately slapped her back to consciousness (thank God I knew what I was doing) and her whole body was spasming and she looked back at me disoriented and confused.

She first asked me how long she was out, and I told her that it was just a second or two. She gathered herself for a moment, and then told me that it was amazing and that she came harder than she had ever come in her life. I know never to trust the flatterings of a puta, but to my credit her body was still shaking and she wanted me to hold her like a purring kitten for a really long time.

I told her I wanted to see her again, and that there were things on my list that I still haven't done to her. We made an appointment to meet up at 3am when her shift ended, so she wouldn't have to worry about me ruining her makeup…

So I after that first session, I went back downstairs to HK and met back up with my wingman, We hung out and objectively rated the face and bodies of the chicas, but really I was just letting my loads regenerate and waiting for the big showdown at 3am.

3am rolled around and Dilan texted me like clockwork and we went up to my room again. Right away, she told me she wanted me to face fuck her and ruin her make up. I stood on bed, grabbed a handful of her hair, spat on her face, then shoved my dick down her throat. She actually wrapped her hands around my ass and held on to the deep throat to the point that she gagged up globs of saliva and mucus. If she had a full stomach she probably would have puked. I threw her down on the bed and smeared the slime she gagged up all over her face, ruining her makeup as promised.

I started to fuck her missionary again, and as I was doing that she grabbed my hand and shoved my fingers down her throat, making me manually gag her. I obliged. She also guided my hands on her carotid arteries and told me to choke her out again, but from the front. I also obliged. It was more fun to choke her out from the front during missionary, because the fucking was not interrupted with her passing out, and it felt great "fucking" her back to consciousness.

Then she said she wanted it in her ass. She first shoved her thumb in her own ass while I was fucking her, then she sucked her thumb. I was so disgusted/turned by the act that I immediately grabbed her by the hair, pulled her head back, told her to open wide, and spat right into her mouth. She swallowed my spit and said, "Thank you, sir."

I exploded like a shotgun.

Now I'm missing some details because we fucked several times and chatted a lot between each session. At one point, we talked about sex toys and how she liked getting fucked with anal beads in her ass, etc. I didn't have any toys with me, but I'm pretty good at improvising. So I unhooked the hotel telephone and used the telephone cord to hog-tie her. She was on her stomach with her hands and feet tied together behind her back. I took a sock out of my bag and shoved it in her mouth. Then looked around and saw that I had a bag of peanut M&Ms I bought earlier. I emptied the bag of M&Ms into a condom, and started shoving it, bead by bead, into her ass until the entire condom containing a full bag of M&Ms was in her ass.

I had to take a step back and take in the scene as a whole after that. There she was, hog-tied, writhing and wriggling, with mascara running down her face, a sock in her mouth, and a bag of M&Ms in her ass. I was so turned on by the sight that I took a running start, diving back into bed to fuck her again. I had to undo the hog-tie and took the sock out of her mouth so I could fuck her from behind with her stomach flat on the bed. I kept the bag of M&Ms in her ass though. After we were done, she pulled the M&Ms-filled condom out of her ass, untied the condom, and ate a few of them.

She didn't leave until dawn, and a lot of other stuff happened too. But I have to keep some details to myself!

Bullshitting the Bullshitter: PLM Pulls the Ultimate Scam

Maverick

It was 2006 and CC was still a happening place with good quality. I was on a PSE roll with dancers Damaris, Wendy, Jenny de GDL, and Alma, so I was frequenting the place quite often. Anyway, there was another hot blonde working at the time: Kenya, about 5'7", thin, fake tits, nice nose job, with a Paris Hilton haircut. In fact, she looked like Paris Hilton, only prettier with a better body. Kenya had white skin and could pass for a hot gringa more than a Latina. She never got onto my personal radar screen because she was too tall for me (I'm only 5'7" and self conscious about it), but I think she was a very hot chica who'd been around the block. I guess she was in her mid-20s but the plastic surgery told me she'd made good money over her career. She could also speak very good English so she was no FOB.

Anyway, a long-time business associate of mine was going through a mid-life crisis and gravitated toward hanging out in Zona Norte in an attempt to cure it. This guy was—and still is—a good friend with a good heart. He's a bit goofy and has zero game when it comes to operating in the P4P arena, but he likes the diversion it offers. I'll call the guy "Hef" since he once told me he wanted to be the "Hugh Hefner of TJ." (I told you he was goofy.)

Hef had, and still has, a very good cash flow and is not hurting in the money department. But he didn't have many friends, and so he began a business guiding motorcycle tours into northern Baja as a way to meet and make new friends.

It was a stupid idea that didn't go very far, but he managed to get about four interested callers over a one-year period. Each of the guys was a lonely-hearted type who was new in town and looking for something social to do. The tours didn't advertise Zona Norte but once the question of fun came up, it usually became all about the sex.

Within a few months, Hef had four trip buddies who were all single, unattached guys looking for love, with zero experience in dealing with Mexico and Zona Norte. It was a disaster in the making, and I can tell story after story of how they were eaten up by the TJ sharks. But I'll focus on Claude, who actually turned out to be the shark.

Claude was 44, fat, sweaty, and looked like a human Polish sausage. Actually, I used to refer to him as "Big Pussy" because he looked exactly like that character from *The Sopranos*, only more disheveled. The only thing I was told about Claude's life was that he'd been in the Navy. Claude had tagged along with one of the guys who'd responded to the Baja bike tour ad. He didn't have any money but was allowed to come along because he was driving one of the guy's chase cars that they kept all their gear in. At the end of the ZN trip, I guess Claude and Hef became buddies and whenever I had business at Hef's office, Claude would be there hanging around. I didn't know it at that time, but Claude had told Hef that he was a trust fund baby who was waiting for 10 million dollars to get released to him upon his 45th birthday.

During my trips to Tijuana, I would occasionally run into this "Lonely Hearts Club" that was always in CC as they quickly developed their favoritas. Claude wound up with Kenya and he quickly took a permanent liking to her. I think she was his one and only puta.

Fast forward several months, and I saw the "Club" members in CC and sat down for a drink with them. Claude was with Kenya, and he got up to take a piss. Kenya told me, "I love this man, I don't care about his money; he has a good heart." I recall laughing because I figured he must have told her he was rich, when to look at him he was just an average slob. I still hadn't heard about his "trust fund." The other guys did tell me he was ass-fucking her and of course BB, and from what she just said, I had no reason to doubt it.

Before I knew it, Hef reported that there were wedding plans in effect. By this time, I had heard about Claude's trust fund and hadn't given it two thoughts. I couldn't have cared less about him or even Hef, who was a big boy who had his own life.

Then one day Hef asked me some legal questions about how a beneficiary could break a trust. But once I began asking questions about the trust, I knew something was funny. Hef explained that Claude stood to inherit between seven and fifteen million dollars that was in a trust for his benefit, but his brother was the trustee and did not want to release the funds. I told Hef it was a simple matter, that the trustee is obligated by law to release the funds if that's what the trust says.

Then I started getting a story about this and that, and I told him to get it in writing or consider it bullshit. None of it made any sense. How many sailors come from uber-rich millionaire families? Aren't most trust funds set to release funds upon the age of majority or completion of college, etc.? This douchebag was 44 years old!

Soon I learned from Hef that he had been supporting him on the promise that Claude would give him control over financial planning and could live off interest on the investment income, etc. Hef was planning to quit his business based on this BS.

Mid-life crisis; stupidity abounds…

I was 100% convinced that Claude was penniless and a scam artist, but Hef told me I was just an antisocial asshole always talking shit about people. He was at least right about that. Needless to say, I never got invited to the wedding, but later that month, I showed up at Hef's birthday party and got to see Claude showing everyone the photos.

The wedding was at Las Rocas in Rosarito and Kenya looked great. She had several bridesmaids. I assume they were all putas, although I did not recognize any of them except Perla de Sinaloa. Kenya promptly retired from the puta business and awaited her appointment for her green card.

With wedding complete (paid for in full by Hef, I later learned), the happy couple was living together in TJ awaiting her INS interview. I saw them come into CC one night and talk to someone, then get into an argument, and leave. I later learned from Claude's buddy that Kenya wanted some cocaine and tried to get some from her friend but he couldn't produce. Made perfect sense. I became intrigued at what was going on in their lives… kind of like watching the Kardashians, where you know they're pathetic but you just want to see how stupid people can be.

Claude's buddy (not Hef, but another guy—another totally innocent and gullible friend) became a bit lonely when Kenya stole his best friend and he was never at a loss for words telling me what was going on in their lives. I learned that Kenya had gone and looked at some new condos in Cacho and wanted to move in, but they settled on something more modest, much to her disapproval. This was solely to wait for her visa.

Claude was still trying to break the trust free from evil brother's control with the help of Hef. Kenya was getting pissed at having to live as a commoner and was running out of patience waiting for the money to come in. Kenya told Claude she had a grandmother in Tecate who was dying and needed cash. After complaining and crying, Claude got the cash together. Then Kenya needed more money for something else, and Claude couldn't pay the bill. She threatened to go back to work, and Claude miraculously came up with it. Nobody knew it, but time was running out.

Several months had gone by and the couple was still awaiting the INS interview in Juarez. Claude and Hef were still battling the evil brother with nasty phone calls, faxes, etc. As some point in the fighting, Claude was kicked out of his own apartment in TJ and forced to live on the friend's couch. One day, the friend does some banking and realizes someone had stolen some checks out of his checkbook and cashed them. In five minutes, he had Claude pegged. He called the cops. Claude was questioned and admitted he just borrowed some cash. The detectives did a little digging and learned that he had also been stealing his mother's Social Security checks and cashing them as well. Claude was charged with several felonies and given a court date for arraignment. (FYI, on most non-violent felonies where the defendant is cooperative, prosecutors generally do not do an arrest but will allow him to show up in court on his own recognizance.)

I heard the news from Hef and I didn't bat an eye. When he told me about the court date, I just laughed with the "I told you so" grin.

How much had Hef loaned Claude?

$20,000!!

(Hef is very successful and can live without that cash, a fact he continually reminds me of).

Anyway, the next thing I learned from Hef was that Claude never made it to court. The cops found him dead inside a Motel 8 in Point Loma, the victim of an apparent suicide via pill overdose. No note was left.

The news hit Kenya pretty hard. She kept pestering Hef with phone calls about why she could not come to the funeral, saying she would promise to go back to Mexico afterwards. She couldn't understand why her deal to come to the US was gone. After a while, she stopped calling him.

A year later, I saw Kenya working in AB. She looked good. She saw me. I looked at her and laughed. She walked out of the club alone and never returned that night.

Now I must digress for a moment. Kenya hated me because she knew that I thought her prince was a douchebag. She also thought I was an asshole from prior experience. One night, I was sitting with Damaris, and Kenya came and sat to talk to her about something. The waiter comes and asks her, not me, if she wants a drink, and she says yes. Drink comes and she is oblivious. Waiter looks at me and I pay, not wanting to create a scene with my BB honey Damaris. Then Kenya gets up to leave and doesn't even acknowledge the drink or me. That was too much.

I called her back and said, "The next time you order a drink at my table and don't pay for it, you'd better ask me first." I did not say it politely either.

She blew up and screamed she'd pay, left and returned with seven bucks, which she slammed down on the table.

I asked, "What about the tip?" But she didn't hear that as she stormed off. Of course, Damaris told me I was cheap and not being nice.

I never saw Kenya again but Claude's buddy told me he found her on MySpace or something and it looked like she met another Prince Charming. She has never been back to the zone in a working capacity, so I am sure some monger snatched her up. She would be a great trophy wife if you could put up with her addictions to money and drugs.

One final note: both of the victims I referred to, the buddy and Hef, have no ill will toward Claude. They are bummed that he lied and both told me they would have given him the money if he really needed it. I guess the moral of the story from their perspective is certain vulnerable people see what they want to see. Those guys wanted a trip buddy/friend so badly they looked past the obvious warning signs to get and keep one.

And to the guy who is currently fucking Kenya: I salute you. She looks like a great fuck. My guess is she now lives in the US and is driving a BMW 3 series.

A FOB Slobbed My Knob

ELNIQUE

My plan was to place some Super Bowl bets at Caliente, and then head back to the US and go to the Nike Outlet to purchase a b-day gift.

6:09pm I arrive at Caliente, place my bets, and head out the door. As I'm leaving, I hear the Zona calling my name. I tried to ignore her calls but La Zona pleaded and became more persistent. I eventually gave in.

6:21pm I jumped in a Taxi Libre (50pesos) and got dropped off near Adelita. I was in a serious time crunch and knew tonight I needed to be decisive and was wise with my time. I immediately took a quick lap around the zone and took some mental notes. I was pleasantly surprised at the number of SGs out on a Wednesday evening in late January.

6:34pm I started to do another lap when the aroma of the taco stand near Play Boy hit me. I ordered two tacos de adobada (40p) and scarfed them down then continued my second lap. While walking up the hill right before Bar Reno, I notice a chica in a red dress that I've never seen before. I chat her up. Her name is Laura from Veracruz. She seems shy and talks quietly. I decide to take her to the hotel.

6:50pm As we ascend the steps of Hotel Rio Nilo, Laura looks back twice to see if I'm still there. She seems sort of hesitant as we reach the entrance. The hotel reeks of freshly sprayed roach killer.

I pay the hotel clerk 80 pesos for 15 minutes in the room. When we reach the room, I ask Laura how long has she's been in TJ. She says, "A week." Her dress was a little shabby and her nail polish almost non-existent. If I had to take a wild guess, she probably used most of the little money she had to get to TJ. She asked my age and I asked hers (21).

Right before we begin our session, she asks, "If it's 6:52 now, what time will it be in 15 minutes?" I jokingly tell her 9:30. She laughs and then I tell her 7:07. I'm thinking to myself that she might actually be new to this line of work.

The Veracruz vixen undresses. Her body is not banging, but she does have some knockers and a decent booty. I get a CBJ. She has good skills and it was nothing like one of those robotic run-of-the-mill BJs. The only thing I didn't like was she periodically would look at the condom to see if I came. Overall good, though. Great attitude in the room, nice personality. I would repeat. Spewed at 7:04pm. I had a watch on. (200p service; 20p + $3 tip)

7:08pm Depart the Zona on foot. As I'm walking to the crossing, I notice a Haitian restaurant near the Bienvenidos Tijuana sign across the street from the police station. I have major respect for these Haitian people who seem to make the best of whatever situation they are in no matter what their circumstances are.

7:31pm Cross back into the US. Zero wait time. I walk over to Plaza America purchase the gift. Mission accomplished.

Duration of visit: 1hour 23min
Money Spent: 390p and $3
(My shortest and least expensive trip to LZ
in my mongering career!)

I Was Robbed!

SMD

I stayed last week at the Hacienda de Santiago (aka the HDS) and was enjoying my usual cheapo good times with BBBJs and BBFS sessions with a lot of the chicas that I now regularly cita with.

Before any of my regulars spotted me on the street, I offered Lorena 100p for a simple BJ when I saw her close to the Tecate beer corner. She started my week off with a very lame and very short BBBJ. After only 5 or 6 minutes she started making sounds like she was exhausted, so I asked her for poquito mas, and maybe got 2 more minutes before I said she was fini. I only tipped her one regalo item and sent her on her way.

Later that day when asked who I'd seen already, I separately informed Letti, then Norma, and eventually Elizabeth of the lame BJ Lorena gave. The first words out of each of their mouths were, "Lorena es loco."

One thing in particular that I enjoyed during this trip at the HDS was having chicas walk in while I was in the middle of fucking someone else. Maybe five or six times this week I was balls deep in a chica when the house phone rang. I excused myself from chica #1 to answer the phone. The HDS front desk would tell me that chica #2 was downstairs and I would tell them to let #2 cum up. I would then unlock the door and resume fucking chica #1. When chica #2 knocked on my door, I would yell "Entrada" and then look at the shocked faces of various chica #2s as they entered the room. Later in the week when Elizabeth asked about this particular practice, I smiled and admitted that I was twisted in this way.

The big event of this trip began on what was supposed to be the last (7th) night. I had finished fucking Letti in a cita where I did not pop. As soon as she left, I showered and then walked out onto the street to see whom I might use for that late evening pop I wanted. Standing in front of the Adelita clothing store at 2am was a spinner type of light-skinned chica that I had never seen before. Her stomach looked as if it might be blown out, but otherwise she looked ideal for my superflaca tastes. The name she gave me was Estephanie. I offered her 100 pesos for a blowjob and we immediately headed to the top floor of the HDS. Before we began our session, she agreed to a picture with all her clothes on.

Her BBBJ skills and performance were average and she indicated that she wanted to fuck, but with a condom. So I pulled one out of the night stand. Her fucking motions were a little herky-jerky and I was tired. It was late in an exhaustive week. My Viagra doses for the day had occurred too many hours earlier and, with all that happening, I was softening up.

At one point, to keep things progressing, Estephanie took off the condom, blew me up again, and then let me resume fucking her, but this time without a condom. We went at it for a long time, and then during a short pause in the action, she began snoring. I tried gently waking her a couple of times, but she stayed asleep. So I covered her up with a flannel blanket, did my hydrogen peroxide treatment, and I then laid awake the whole rest of the night in the other bed.

Renata was scheduled to arrive at 8am the next morning, and she did. I pointed out the chica still sleeping in the bed and suggested that we wake her by each of us kissing Estephanie on opposite face cheeks. (Only on TJAmigos is it necessary to include the word "face" in the prior sentence.)

But when we planted our simultaneous kisses on Estephanie, she pulled the flannel blanket tightly over her head. So Renata and I just fucked without her in the contiguous bed. At the end of fucking Renata, I paid Renata while she selected her regalo, and then bid Renata adieu.

Figuring that this new Estephanie was going to keep sleeping for a while, maybe even close to checkout, I had to make a decision.

And like many decisions I was going to make this Friday, it was the wrong one.

I decided to rent the room for one more night. So while new Estephanie continued to sleep, I went down to the front office and paid 565 pesos to take the room for one more night.

Ratera Estephanie continued to sleep as Elizabeth stopped by. She grabbed a juice box and we talked. Then Norma and Fannie/Estephanie also stopped by, and they also had some fruit juice. Then Letti and Alejandra came a knockin', and all six of us for a moment were drinking fruit juices, talking, and looking at the sleeping chica.

Fortunately I was in one of HDS' biggest rooms. Soon after Letti and Alejandra left, Ratera Estephanie suddenly woke up and sprang naked out of the bed. RE looked around, appearing a little puzzled to be surrounded by these three other chicas. I grabbed a fruit juice box out of the refrigerator for RE as she draped herself in the flannel blanket.

At times, both Norma and RE were rubbing or leaning against me. Each of these two alpha chicas sat in my lap at times, but they weren't politely taking turns. In fact, Norma and RE had "words" with each other with enough fire that Elizabeth suggested that I get rid of this new girl.

I looked at Elizabeth, smiled and said, "You're right. There are just too many Stephanies in the room right now."

During the next few uneasy minutes there were several

suggestions made to me to unload this new Estephanie... from all quarters... and I wish I had taken the advice. I did decide to pay RE 200 pesos and tell her that she could pick two items out of the regalo box, which she did.

And yes, I should have escorted Ratero Estephanie to the door about then.

But instead, I sat down on the bed and I made everyone an offer using Elizabeth as the translator to help me make my pitch. I said, "Now normally with you ladies, I will pay each of you 100 pesos to take turns sucking me. But I want to do something different this morning. I still want to do the regular sucki-sucki-sucki thingy. But I want to videotape it. And for that I am willing to pay 200 pesos to each chica that participates." Elizabeth repeated my offer to everyone in Spanish.

Norma immediately accepted; Fannie/Estephanie immediately declined. Elizabeth said that she was game, but cautioned me that she did threesomes, but not foursomes.

I think Ratera Estephanie may have initially shook her head. Then Ratera Estephanie accepted my offer with a smile.

Elizabeth reminded me of her limits and said she was now out of the action.

I placed two small tables near the beds, positioned the two cameras at 90-degree angles from each other, and started the cameras. Elizabeth and Fannie/Estephanie left and I jumped on the beds.

Norma began sucking me as Ratera Estephanie wandered around the room, occasionally dancing to the music.

So the "BBBJ threesome" on video did not go very well.

Ratera Estephanie wouldn't take either my nor Norma's instruction very well. Only with an inordinate amount of coaxing on my part did she eventually return to the bed. And when she did, she danced on the bed above both Norma and I.

In the end, RE doused herself and me in lubricant and proceeded to slip and slide all over me instead of sucking me off.

Norma got frustrated and got dressed. I paid her and she left.

Now it was just me and RE alone in the room. She started play-acting that we were going to pack up the room and leave.

RE pranced around the room and began "pretending" that she was packing things up. First she grabbed the regalo box that by this time was fairly well depleted and dumped its contents into a duffle bag of mine. (At this point, it contained mostly just mini flashlights, packs of Sheriff cigarettes, and about eight bottles of garish nail polishes.) The duffle bag was a yellow and purple canvas bag from LSU that had a large illustration of their tiger mascot.

RE went through the room and kitchen, placing all items into either the LSU bag, the banker's box that had served as the regalo box, or a very large plastic bag from Daiso (the Japanese store where I buy some of the regalo items). I was mostly amused by her actions at this point. If I had been paying closer attention, I would have noticed that all the electronics and high value items were going into the LSU bag.

Hours ago, I had securely stored my laptop elsewhere, but into the LSU bag went my cellphone, my old 3rd generation iPod, and the chargers for my phone, computer, and other equipment that needed to be charged. She also placed in the bag two of my four-color "disco" lightbulbs and all three of the remotes I possessed in the room. Then she picked up one of the two identical red Vivitar cameras and began looking at the images it contained.

I grabbed it from her just after she deleted its contents. I removed the SD card and placed the camera down as we both reached for the other camera. I came up with it and immediately removed the SD card.

Stupid me was FINALLY starting to get concerned with this bitch's behavior. After getting dressed, she put both cameras in the LSU bag and then added the space heater to that bag. This made the contents of the LSU bag too much to zip it closed.

I put on my shorts under my robe and flip-flops and paid RE another 200 pesos for her unstructured video performance as I told her it was time for her to go. I noticed she had placed the LSU bag, the bankers box, and the Daiso bag all close to the door.

When I picked up the banker's box and moved it away from the door, she grabbed the LSU bag and darted out the door. I ran after her.

I chased her down all four flights of stairs yelling, "NO! NO! NO!"

If I'd have had the presence of mind to kick off my flip-flops, I probably would have caught her on the stairs.

Hotel guests heard the noise I was making and came out of their rooms to look at the spectacle of me chasing her in my bathrobe down the stairs.

I yelled extra loud as we approached the ground level. I expected Francisco to catch her in the lobby… but the lobby appeared empty as I saw her run out the front door of the HDS.

A few seconds after she ran out the front door, Francisco entered the lobby through the same front door and said that policia were in the area. He suggested that I wait in the lobby, which I did for a while. Blanca was at the front desk through the entire incident.

But after waiting for a while, with nothing apparently happening, I went back up to my room to secure it (I had left it unlocked). About ten minutes later, Francisco and a policia field supervisor came up to my room. The supervisor asked me what was taken. I told him most of the contents I remembered. He said that they caught the girl on the street just outside of the hotel and she was going to jail. The policia supervisor asked me if I needed any of my stuff right away.

I replied that the bag contained the charger to my laptop, which I would need back eventually, but I didn't immediately need it. At this point, I didn't realize that my cellphone was also in the LSU bag. That supervisor never told me to go with him, or that I needed to press charges. He just left after repeating that they were going to take her to jail.

Francisco later said the policia had indeed caught the chica and placed her in the back of the police car, then left. Francisco thought she had been arrested. A few hours later, I walked to the police facility on Madero (near the pedestrian walkway) to ask about my stuff, but they said they could not help me without the name of the policeman I had talked with, which I hadn't retained. They suggested that I go to the police building next to the arch.

When I went there, they said basically the same thing, that I needed the policeman's name. They suggested that I go back to my hotel and call the police using #066. So I went back to the HDS and enjoyed a couple of sessions with my regulars. They were pissed that I had been ripped off by Ratera Estephanie, especially since that chica had stolen the remaining regalo items that were held in my closet!

After the chicas left, I went downstairs and talked to Francisco. Francisco said that after six hours, the chica would be released from jail and that she would then return to the HDS and return my stuff. I thought that sounded pretty odd, but he insisted that was how things worked in La Zona.

I said the policia told me to call 066 about the incident, but he said I couldn't call that number from the hotel; he even had me try to from the front desk, to no avail. So I sat down in the HDS lobby for about an hour and waited to see if any more of my freelancers would stop by.

When it got to be six and a half hours after the grab-and-run, I again went to Francisco and said his earlier suggestion of the return of my stuff was not happening since it was now past six hours since the theft and arrest. Francisco told me that I would now need to go to the jail and he gave me sketchy directions as to where the jail was. After a few wrong turns, I found the jail.

At the main desk, I explained what happened that afternoon

and that I was there to claim my bag and stuff. I was led back down a corridor to another interior desk. It seemed like maybe it was a dispatch desk with a policeman and two policewomen answering phones and working with desktop computers. A large sign above this interior desk read "Barandilla Operativa."

This policia officer heard my story and he spent a lot of time checking that day's arrest records. He even went in the back to look at records from some second source. He declared that they had no record of any arrest between 2 and 3pm in the area of the HDS. He struggled for the correct words to give me and ultimately uttered that policia corruption might have been the reason for no arrest. He said that a big problem with police corruption existed in the area around the HDS.

He encouraged me to come back at 6pm the next day to see if I could identify the cop that I spoke to. He grabbed a sheet of paper and wrote "6:00 P.M." on it and handed it to me and told me and told me to come back tomorrow. He said the same cops from the same shift working that same Zona area would all be there at 6pm at the end of their shift, and I could then identify the policeman that I talked to. I asked the dispatcher guy for his name. I handed him back the sheet of paper and had him write his name on it. I then drove back to the HDS for another night of debauchery.

The prior night when Ratera Estephanie was sleeping, I had e-mailed her picture to my quasi-wingman who responded with his usual criticism of RE's ugly looks and he encouraged me to increase my chica budget.

I realized I could print the emailed photo of RE so I went to the internet cafe and printed two black and white pictures of Miss Ratero. I gave one of the pics to the HDS front desk because they asked for her pic. I kept the second copy in my room, on display for all the chicas that stopped by for a juice and a cita during the next morning and afternoon. Both Renata and Norma said that they planned to beat RE up if they ever saw her again.

Elizabeth stopped by my room at 5pm the next afternoon. At around 5:20, the house phone rang. I told the desk to let Renata come on up. Then I unlocked my room's door and resumed fucking Elizabeth. When Renata arrived she immediately stripped and jumped into the bed to join us. She didn't even stop for a juice! But I did ask her to set an alarm on her cellphone for 5:40pm. Once in bed I happily fucked them both. After a while, as we were positioning ourselves for my 4-handed finish, the alarm rang.

I paid the girls and jumped in the shower to clean myself off while they shopped their respective reserve regalo bags pulled from the closet. They each wanted a slice of the remaining Mexican cheesecake, so I suggested that they spilt the remainder of the pie and take it to go.

At 5:50pm, we rode the elevator down together. When we hit the lobby there was an elderly guy that maybe had just checked in. He looked at the three of us, the girls with regalo filled bags hanging from one shoulder while their other hands each held up chocolate syrup over cheesecake slices and declared "Now THAT's how to do things!" I patted him on his shoulder as we walked by.

Both girls gave me parting kisses in the parking lot. They left and I jumped in my car. The dash clock said the time was 5:52. So I barely had enough time to hit the first information desk at the jail by 5:59. I held up the paper that had 6:00 P.M. and the dispatcher's name written on it. The receptionist went back and brought the male dispatcher with her.

He looked at me, smiled, and then checked some type of appointment list they had at the front desk. He said "Yes, 6:00 o'clock," and he escorted me back to his dispatcher's desk. He had me wait in the same area where I had talked to him the prior night. So I leaned against the solid wall.

The area behind the dispatch desk was a very busy area. It held about nine or ten cops. Other cops continuously entered and exited that area from all these different hallways and entrances. As

I stood there waiting, I probably saw over 30 different cops enter and exit the area directly behind the dispatch desk. Gradually that area swelled to contain around 15 cops.

By himself, the cop who met me in my HDS room entered from the right and parked himself behind this large group of policia. I recognized him immediately. After a few minutes about five or six cops exit to the left, and my guy walked off to right.

The dispatcher came out from behind his desk. "Did you see the policeman that talked to you?" he asked.

"Yes, he was the only guy that just now entered and exited from the right. That bigger group of police all came and went from the left."

He asked if I was sure, and I said yes. The dispatcher then went into the back and walked back to me with that officer. The remainder of that area behind the dispatch desk once again swelled with officers, but this time most of them were staring directly at me and holding their glaring stares.

The two of them stepped from behind the desk, and we conduct our conversation right there. Dispatcher guy and I speak in English to each other and the cop I fingered spoke only in Spanish, and only to dispatcher guy.

In Spanish, the dispatcher guy was telling the cop the details of my story and he went into a good amount of details, including specifically mentioning the items that were in my bag. Then dispatcher guy turned to me:

> *Are you sure this is the police officer that you met yesterday?*
>
> *Yes.*
>
> *Are you sure?*
>
> *Yes.*
>
> *And he's the one you spoke to in your room?*
>
> *Yes.*

In Spanish?

No, in English.

He spoke to you in English?

Yes.

Do you see any other policeman that were there at your hotel around 2 o'clock when the theft happened?

No, I never saw any other policia yesterday, only this man.

This man is a supervisor. Are you sure it was him that you met?

Yes, but I would like for him to speak in a little in English, so I can identify his voice and be even more certain.

No, he's not going to do that. He's a supervisor… are you really sure it was him that talked to you?

Like I said, I would like to hear his voice speaking English.

That's not possible, he does not speak English.

I thought to myself… *BULLSHIT!!!* I think every cop in Tijuana speaks English, some better than others, and this guy appeared to be just fair at best in English when we met the day before.

But I decided to play along with this outright lie and said the following when I looked directly at the cop I identified. "I'm sorry. I must have misidentified you. I apologize. You look exactly like the policia I talked to in mi cuartos, but if you don't speak English, I must be mistaken. The policeman I met with yesterday looks just like you do, but he knew English and talked to me in English."

I then turned and faced dispatcher guy and apologized to him. Dispatcher guy said, "Don't leave just yet. Please stay just a little bit longer and if you don't mind, please stand over there. There's another officer I want you to meet and talk to, he will have more questions for you."

Every time I was asked to wait—and that happened a lot this night—I was left standing by myself for a good 10 to 15 minutes, usually under the glaring stares of a dozen or more sets of eyes.

Dispatcher guy finally brings this other policeman to meet me. His uniform is different than all the other policia. He has no name badge and he is wearing this thick vest that is canvas covered. The vest is sort of like an office organizer, with holders for pens, pencils, a small writing pad and a loop on the bottom. He has a set of handcuffs clipped to it at the bottom, slightly above his belt line. This policeman I will call a "cop in vest" (or CIV) and I notice another policeman dressed just like him standing behind me as he interviewed me so we'll call them all CIV. The main gist of his interview was to again get to my assertion that I could make a good identification of the policia that spoke to me and getting a lot more details of my stolen items. We spoke for a long time.

Every now and then the police supervisor I had fingered out would reappear in the area behind the dispatch desk. He would talk to other police personnel and occasionally stare at me. I always made it a point of staring back at him and never looking away. During these long waits, I noticed there were just a few more of these cops in vests with no name tags and they, along with dispatcher guy, were always carefully watching me as I had these stare downs with the fingered cop. I was out to demonstrate that I was not going to back down under any amount of pressure, and they seemed to be grinning about that fact, unlike the other policia that were just giving me cold hard stares.

There were two sets of interviews with the main cop in vest, where he asked the same questions repeatedly. He chuckled after he asked me if I spoke Spanish and my answer to him was, "Not in sentences." Main CIV said that he wanted me to follow him in his vehicle back to the HDS.

At HDS, the main CIV interviewed Blanca. They talked a long time, with Blanca doing most of the talking for long stretches. She apparently saw a lot of what happened. After interviewing Blanca, the main CIV seemed content with Blanca's information and he told me that he wanted me to follow him to the jail in my car.

Once we arrived at the jail again, this main CIV introduced me to a cop that appeared to be of a high rank. He had the same prominent badges on his shoulder as did the fingered cop. He said that he was a supervisor. This supervisor's name was Hernandez.

The main CIV talked to Hernandez at first, giving him a rundown, then Hernandez interviewed me with much of the same questions along with asking me a lot about my background. Hernandez was the first policeman to ask me for identification, so I handed him my passport. After interviewing me for a long time, he asked me to wait again.

So I had another long wait, complete with stares from the police milling about behind the dispatch desk and the occasional appearance and staredown from fingered cop. After another long wait, I was introduced to El Jefe Valencia.

El Jefe Valencia asked me the same series of questions, with an emphasis challenging that I was sure that I had identified the right cop. He was also particular in questioning my Spanish skills and my assertion that fingered cop had talked to me in English the prior day at HDS.

Valencia then wanted me to me to go back with him to the HDS. I arrived at HDS at the same time some of the other officers were arriving. I went up to my room and grabbed the one remaining copy I had of the picture of Ratera Estephanie. The moment I joined the group of policia on the sidewalk in front, Hernandez asked me why I went up to my room.

I told him that I went up to get a picture of the girl and handed him the printed photo. He seemed shocked that I had a picture of RE to give him, and it was quickly passed around to all six officers as we all stood in a circle on the sidewalk immediately outside the entrance to HDS. Hernandez kept RE's picture, as he was the only officer that had report papers and was taking notes.

Valencia asks me yet again to confirm that the fingered

supervisor spoke to me in English and then, to test my correct identification, he asked me if I could describe the man I had identified just one hour earlier. I said yes, then described his build, shape and length of his moustache, the style and length of his hair, and then I said he was easily distinguishable on that day and the prior day by the cold blister on his lower lip.

He acted like he did not understand exactly what I meant by the word blister, so I pointed to exact spot were it appeared and said it was a small oval with white discolorization on the front of his lip. Valencia still seemed puzzled by what I was saying until one of the CIVs put his own finger up to his own lip and said "huevos," which caused all the officers to chuckle. Valencia once again asked me if the fingered supervisor had spoken to me in English, with almost a unbelieving expression on his face (as if that dirty supervisor doesn't speak English).

He then pointed across the street to a policia car and asked me if I could identify that squad car or the two police officers that were leaning against the vehicle. The vehicle and new officers were parked right in front of La Tropa. I said no, but added that I never saw any other policemen on the day of the theft, just the supervisor that I identified. I told them all that the only person I knew that had seen the officers with the ratera was Francisco, the HDS security guy. The problem was that Francisco was not at the hotel since it was his day off.

Just as it seemed they might be done questioning me, a call came over their police radios. I guess it was important and urgent, since all of them jumped in their various official vehicles, ran sirens, and peeled out southbound on Revolución.

I sat down in the HDS lobby thinking about what had just transpired when the main CIV walked back into the HDS lobby. He apparently hadn't left with the other officers. It was Saturday. He asked me if I was leaving at the end of the weekend. I said that was my original plan, but I could stick around longer in TJ if it would help. He said "Yes, it would be good if you are available on Monday, to maybe answer some more questions."

I told him that I would stay in TJ, and then he left.

There's only a little more that happened in the following days of the extended trip, other than me hunkering down in the HDS with my crew of freelancers frequently dropping in. My crew treated me like a hero... after all, no group of persons in the Zona gets victimized more by the policia than the unlicensed chicas. When I said that to Elizabeth, she agreed and she said that the policia are always hitting up her and the other freelancer girls to give them free sex.

"What? I thought the cops would just pop you ladies for 200 pesos so you could work and not be hassled any more that night."

"They make us give BOTH the 200 pesos and the free sex, those bastards!" Liz replied.

Whenever I was out on the street anytime during the remainder of my trip (and I tried not to make that happen much), I was completely paranoid, looking carefully at every policia, even though they all seemed oblivious to my existence. Ortiz came driving by the HDS in one of those high profile 4-seat pickups. Another CIV was riding shotgun. This day they were not wearing their vests, but they also still did not have on name tags. I was walking Renata in for a cita. Ortiz motioned me to come over to him curbside and talk to him. So I stepped away from Renata to talk to him and the other CIV. Ortiz said that he wanted to talk to me some more, but it looked like I was busy. I said that I was always busy, but we could talk now. He suggested, "Later? Maybe in half an hour?"

I looked at Renata and said "Well, what about an hour?"

He said "Fine, one hour," but he never made another appearance.

By the time I left for the USA on Tuesday, I was largely over my paranoia and comfortable with being in and around the Zona again. But as always, I still walk around with very little dinero, and keep my head on a constant swivel. My current trip started nine days after this trip ended. This week I've been back in La Zona a lot and it's almost as if I'm invisible to every policia I come across.

If anything else happens to me, it most likely will be when I least expect it.

Maddog's Adventure with Kamala

MADDOG

Kamala and I messaged each other for a few days before we finally decided to make a date. It was for a short time session with her picking me up in the morning and me leaving that evening. As you will learn it ended up getting extended. Now she's very adventurous and willing to experiment and try different things and from the tone of our conversation it was decided that she was going to be my little sex slave and I her master for this adventure. Thus I had to make sure that my bag of tricks was adequately supplied with gadgets from the adult toy store before making my trip. And it was.

Now honestly, I was a bit apprehensive about crossing the border carrying a bag like mine. The last thing I wanted was to push that Mexican customs button and have it come up red and then seeing the expressions on the agents' faces while being asked just what I planned to do with the wrist and ankle restraints, 12" g-spot finder rubber dildo with attached anal beads, the blindfold, vibrators, cat-o'-nine tails, assorted lubes, condoms, and cameras, etc. Not to mention the whipped cream, maraschino cherries, chocolate syrup, and vodka. The thought of a quick payoff crossed my mind if it happened, being that I couldn't bear the stares from tourists walking by and shaking their heads at some gringo pervert with all this stuff laid out in the open on the examination table and me probably getting a cavity search.

Luckily for me, it was early in the day and there was only one female customs agent working and she was busily involved rifling through some other poor soul's luggage. So I briskly walked on by and never even pushed the evil button. Made it and all was good. Off to the meeting spot.

I'm a little early so I decide to hit one of the nearby farmacias to buy a Cialis. Now I do not suffer from any erectile dysfunction just yet and had never tried Cialis previously, but I kind of got the drift that it may come on handy in keeping up with a nymphomaniac like Kamala. So I buy the pill for $17 and head over to McDonald's to await my chariot.

She ended up being a little late due to supposed traffic. Now typically, I would have immediately and severely scolded a sex slave who disobeyed a direct order. However, she was wearing the exact type of outfit that I had instructed her to, that being a short miniskirt with no panties along with a loose fitting top and no bra. I figured this way I could play with her tits and pussy on our drive to her beach front home in Rosarito. So I let her slide for the time being.

I must admit I was pleasantly surprised by her appearance. Her facial features are beautiful and her body was perfect for my tastes.

So in I get and off to Pleasureville we go. Of course, I immediately got to examining her wares. I pulled up her skirt, revealing a beautiful fully shaven pussy. I tried to finger her love tunnel, but her driving made that difficult, so I concentrated on tweaking her nipples and massaging and playing with her breasts.

I think she was initially taken aback by all this. I mean, she didn't object at all, but seemed a little shy and embarrassed by this strange man just groping and playing with her most private nether regions. After all, we had never personally met each other before and here is some monger animal basically just doing whatever he pleased with her body. But after some small talk and continued fondling, she seemed a bit more receptive to my wandering hands.

We arrived at Casa Kamala around noon and her cleaning lady is still there working away. The place is beautiful, right on the water with a fantastic view. But that's not what I had come for, thus we excuse ourselves to her upstairs bedroom. I wasted no time in grabbing her and giving her a big kiss. She responded receptively and we passionately DFK'd while making our way over to her bed to start playing. I grabbed some toys out of my bag and we undressed as we were getting on top of the bed. I had already decided to set the tone by eating her pussy and licking her clit to try and please her in the belief that doing so would come back tenfold later on during our time together. So I do my thing, which seemed like forever but she seemed to genuinely enjoy. She was also using a vibrator for her ass by this point as I continued to DATY. After what seemed like an eternity, I had to come up for air and let her reciprocate my efforts. I think she enjoyed herself.

Anyways, my turn for her to do some cock sucking while I used toys on her pussy and ass. Kamala is one fantastic cocksucker. Deep throat, lots of licking, ball kissing and sucking, great eye contact, pulls her hair back so that you get the best view available of her doing her work, and she knows exactly how to suck dick until it throbs. If she had teeth, you'd never know it.

The best of all is that she drinks every last drop when you explode into her pretty mouth.

So as she's attending to me, I get that huge rubber dildo out and start abusing her pussy. She was already lubed so I was able to get it in as far as possible (about 2/3rds of the way) and then stick those four anal beads up her ass. I do all this while she is really engulfing my cock. I start to fuck her with the dildo, which is bent about two inches at the top, and twisting and turning it as I pump it in and out of her pussy. Just bringing it out far enough so that the anal beads would pull against the inner walls of her ass opening without letting any pop out and then thrusting the dildo deep into her. This continues for like 15 minutes before I started feeling very light-headed and flushed, probably due to the half of Cialis I took earlier. I instruct her to stop so that I could make a drink and try and make the weird feeling cease.

We stop and head for the front room. She runs around naked a lot so I assumed that I should do the same and follow. Problem was the cleaning lady was still there and I go walking in naked. Enough of that!

I retreat to throw on some clothes and return to the kitchen to make a Stoli and OJ. We sat and had a few drinks, talking for a while as I cleared my head. She asked if I was hungry and I was. She called her taxi driver friend who was picking up the maid and told him to stop and pick up tacos. He arrives shortly with some carne and pork tacos and we eat as he leaves with the maid.

Well, after a few drinks and a little grub I was feeling much better and the Cialis had kicked in as well. One long look at Kamala and I was ready to get down, so back to the bedroom we go; this time for some real raunchy wild heavy sex.

Clothes off in seconds and passionately groping and kissing each other like high school kids in the back of a car. Kamala wastes no time going for my love muscle and begins to caress and stroke it. Didn't take much and I'm at full mast attention. Condom gets applied and she mounts me on top, guiding my cock into her waiting love tunnel. Nice, and she begins to rock back and forth and hump up and down. I'm thrusting my hips up to meet her motion and gain maximum penetration.

The sexy look on her face really turned me on and we soon began to violently fuck like wild rabbits with me roughly grabbing her nipples and manipulating her breasts. Kamala likes her tits played with rough while having sex; it really gets her going.

We go at it like this for some time and then roll to our sides, continuing to fuck each other the entire time. Soon, I'm on top and we're passionately kissing as I drill away with her wrapping her legs around me. The Cialis made me last forever and I could continue as long as I wanted, but she had different plans and wanted to get fucked in her ass. So I dismount and lie back to enjoy the new ride.

Kamala once again places herself on top of me, but this time to guide my cock into her tight asshole. She applied some love lube and eases her ass around my cock. Man, it was tight!

She begins to go through the same motions as earlier; the only difference is now my cock is embedded deep in her ass. I'm abusing her tits and she soon has a vibrator stimulating her pussy and clit. Wild stuff!

It wasn't long before she was literally lying flat on her back with her legs under her humping back and forth to create as much friction between my cock and her poop shoot as possible. A little awkward for an erect penis, but she made it work and we went at it. Then she shifts so once again she's sitting upright with my cock propping her up as I guide her hips up and down allowing my dick to slide in and out of her ass as she's using the vibrator to stimulate her clit and my cock when she placed it inside her pussy. The feeling of the vibrations on the other side of that thin membrane separating her asshole from her pussy was surreal. This was some damn good stuff and I was thoroughly enjoying every minute of it. This woman loves to get fucked in her ass, even more so than her pussy and we must have continued like this for a good 15 or 20 minutes before I finally told her that I wanted her to give me head and finish me off.

So like a good little sex slave she dismounts my cock, removes the rubber, and begins to do her magic. Now we had been going at it in one way or another for a few hours now and I knew that there was quite a build up of love lava ready to erupt at any moment. All I needed was Kamala's expert assistance.

Kamala begins to suck and lick my dick, and nibbling, licking and sucking my swollen balls. Soon she begins to concentrate on some good old-fashioned heavy cock sucking, taking my dick completely in her mouth and in her throat, one hand massaging my quivering and tightening nutsack and then using the other to stroke the base of my cock. Well, needless to say, I couldn't take much more of this and felt the pressure building, my legs trembling and straightening out with toes curling.

Wham!!!

I moaned as I exploded into her mouth and back of her throat. Like a true trooper, she kept sucking away as spurt after spurt of built-up semen filled her mouth and throat. And she swallowed every last drop and sucked my cock completely dry. One fantastic orgasm and my cock was quivering in ecstasy as she finished.

I was one happy man.

We decided to take a break to make another drink and move to the front room where the bondage session was to take place, but that's another story all together…

Beautiful ROB Does Detention

TROLLEYMAN

So I'm a sucker for slender beautiful spinners with perfect skin, the kind who would never look at me in a club in the US but here they not only do they check me out, they chase me down. At least sometimes. At least when I've got money hanging out of my pockets. But it doesn't always work out for me.

I'm at the point in the night when I'm almost done, when horniness and tiredness kind of balance out and I'm not sure whether I want to go upstairs for the girl or the bed. And then I find this dark haired girl, straight long locks, perfect skin. Wow! It nudges me towards wanting to go upstairs because of the girl, so I negotiate. Okay, 80, standard issue.

We don't chitchat. I don't know Spanish; she doesn't know English. No matter. I don't want a conversation; I want to see her naked and thrust about 245 times. Yes, at that point, I know where my finish line is and I'm coming close to falling off the end of the table. So we go. I love watching her long legs and ass swaying in front of me as we go up the stairs. I pay for the room, we go in, and the fun begins, right?

Uh, maybe not.

I try to strip her down and she wants money now.

Never pay up front!

Well, I never do normally, but she has perfect skin and I want to see all of it. The worst that can happen is I get to see a naked chica and she's gonna be perfect, I can tell.

Do I pay? Do I not?

I take my time to see which head prevails. She's pretty insistent and her legs are just awesome. I gotta see more.

So I pay the $80.

She strips.

It's glorious.

I'm hard as a rock just gazing at her. Best $80 I ever spent, except...

She's just tolerating this. And it slowly goes downhill. She wants it to end, and I suddenly realize I want it to end. But I blew $80 on her. It's been 5 minutes. I'm a fool. She doesn't want to do much of anything.

I hop up and say, "Okay, fine. Give me half the money back."

She shakes her head.

"Give me... give me $20 back."

She shakes her head.

"Something?"

And of course the answer is no. She puts her clothes back on.

"Give me SOME of my money back, it's been five minutes."

"No," she refuses. She's dressed and ready to leave.

And I block the doorway. *No.*

I point to my watch. I paid for 30 MINUTES. I don't care WHAT happens, I'm going to get my 30 minutes. So she sits disgustedly on the bed, and I stand there, playing sentry. Not budging.

For 25 minutes.

It's detention, and this brat is going to sit here until I say it's time for her to leave.

She wants to look at her phone.

NO. It's MY 30 minutes.

I could make you get naked, or I could make you just sit here and be miserable. And that I do.

Every minute lasts an eternity. I myself feel like tipping over. But I'm going to get my 30 minutes.

Okay, I give her a break. I keep her only 28 minutes and let her go. This was certainly not my wildest session. I probably could have thought of something more creative for her to do. Like fold my clothing. Clean out my car. Scrub the floors. I may not get sexual satisfaction, but I'm going to get some kind of small twisted satisfaction.

I never realized the thrill my high school teachers felt over being in complete control of the miscreants. What a weird turn-on.

Forbidden Fruit

KENDRICKS

My heart was pounding as her lips slid over my rock-hard cock. She was black, beautiful, with big full tits and a sexy, feminine hardbody. My mind was reeling, and a brutal orgasm was welling up within me. I usually have pretty good dick control, but right now, as I lay in the Hotel Coahuila at 5:10am with an exotic whore ferociously sucking my throbbing rod, I had control of nothing.

It had all started innocently enough. I spent the weekend down in Baja visiting family over the weekend, and my brother-in-law and I decided to go shoot some pool. After a few caguamas, the urge to hit the Zona overtook us.

We started off hitting some Revo titty bars and passed through a number of Zona clubs. La Tropa was surprisingly alive, with a pretty, fully nude dancer on stage when we walked in. All of my in-laws are pretty cool about watching and fondling strippers, but actual whorefucking is a taboo. So, for the time being, I had to make myself content with taking in the scenes, and with some fairly innocent interaction with the girls.

As the night wore on, my desire became harder and harder to control. There are only so many titties a man can feel before he simply must plunge his shaft into a hot, juicy, dripping cunt. Hong Kong, Kaos, Peanuts & Beer... so, so many titties. I repeatedly fell in love during a brief walk through Adelita, but I was unable to do any hunting of my own. We eventually wandered into La Carreta (basically a locals' dive), where I soon found a petite, nice looking 19-year-old sitting next to me. After a drink, the waiter suggested that for $35, I could have a half-hour private show, which included five beers. Sounds good to me… I told my brother-in-law to hang tight, I'd be back to tell him all about the show.

We were escorted to a room in the back with a curtain, table, and two chairs. The five beers were tiny pony beers, but I should have seen that coming. The burning question now: what would the show include?

She grabbed a beer and settled back to talk. I let my hands wander up her tight little legs as I asked her about herself, and she described the sad, sad story of her life. I used to love getting inside the girls' heads, but I'm not so sure about that strategy anymore. She was definitely a cute girl, with a lot of ambition and desire for life in her. She hopes to only work in the bar for long enough to save some cash and pursue her studies. The bar life was hell to her, and she couldn't wait to be done with it. It was now about 4:30am, and my mind was shredded by alcohol, hormones, and frustrated desire.

Self loathing crept in as I groped her body and saw the "deer in headlights" look in her eyes. I backed off, and she told me it was okay; I could touch her. What a ridiculous situation—I'm a 35-year-old man in the middle of a world-famous redlight district, yet I feel like a 16-year-old kid on a first date with a high school sweetie. Absurd.

We passed the time by drinking, kissing, and groping, with no more real action than a little titty sucking, and her feeling my bulging cock through my pants.

After the beers were gone, I thanked her for her time, and went back out to see my bro-in-law. He was getting ready to go back for a private show of his own… excellent!

I was about to be unsupervised in the Zona!!! The thought of burying my dick inside some forbidden fruit was so, so sweet...

I told him I would meet him back at 5:30 and practically ran into the alley, heading straight for Adelita. The superhotties I had lusted after earlier were either gone or occupied.

The depth of my addiction began to disgust me. Here I was on a family trip, obsessing over finding a whore to fuck. *What the hell was wrong with me? Am I really this far gone?*

Then, I had my epiphany. There she was—dark, ebony skin; big full, luscious breasts; a hint of Africano features in her face, and a totally hot hourglass shape. It all made sense now. I had to fuck her.

Usually, I will do some rapport building before making a trip up the stairs. But this morning, rapport meant nothing. I didn't even want to know her name. I just wanted to spread those hardbody legs and plunge my aching cock into her soft, slippery wetness.

"Vámonos arriba?" I asked.

"Sí, por sesenta." (Yes, for $60.)

I counter-offered fifty, she quickly accepted, and we were on our way.

Nervousness overtook me as we entered the room. I'm not sure why; I have definitely fucked my share of whores over the years. Maybe it was the unexpected, yet anticipated satisfaction of pent-up desire. Maybe it was the small window of opportunity I was exploiting. Maybe it was the hours of beer and tequila working on my sometimes unstable psychology. Or perhaps it was just her sweet, chocolate brown skin and big, full tits that were sending waves of adrenaline rushing through my veins.

I quickly shed my clothes and lay back on the bed. She was undressed, and her body was truly blowing my mind. I hadn't fucked a black girl since I had done an American black hooker as a teenager. Every nerve of my body was on edge, desperately waiting for her to grab hold of me. She squeezed some lube into her hand, grabbed my half hard cock, and skillfully worked it into a raging hard-on. She pulled out a high quality condom from her personal stash (God bless her!!! I usually bring my own, since I hate the hotel condoms, but didn't have a supply with me today), professionally wrapped my cock, and clinically wiped off the lube with some tissue.

Just watching her handle my cock was a huge turn-on at this point, but nothing compared to feeling her impale her face on my rock-hard staff. She built up incredible suction and sent waves of pleasure through my body as she bobbed and sucked, while I felt up her big, sweet breasts and her delicious hardbody.

My cum was starting to well up inside me, so I begged her to slow down. *Please, not so quickly, I want to make it last, I want to enjoy every second of it…*

She smiled and looked at me out of the corner of her eyes as she pulled her mouth off my cock, and licked up and down the shaft with the tip of her tongue. The contrast of her smooth, dark skin against my own pasty white body was driving me wild, while her tongue and hands were pushing me over the edge. She expertly switched between full mouth sucking, ball fondling, and shaft and head licking to keep me delicately balanced on the brink, without pushing me over.

Finally she lifted her head from my cock and began to straddle me. I love cowgirl, but I was so close to the brink, I needed some control. I told her to lie on her back, and then spread her legs, and rubbed the head of my hard-on across her sweet, soft lips. I thrust forward, gently working my way inside her tight box.

Her pussy tightly squeezed me as I entered. Once I was fully inside, I lay still for a moment in an effort to acclimate, although I had been pushed so close to the brink that I was bordering on insanity. My skin, my nervous system, my mind, my cock, every fiber of my being was so steeply on edge, I thought my brain was going to explode. I worked my way in and out of her box as it tightly gripped my head and shaft. She smiled at my obvious reaction while I picked up speed, and then I surrendered to my body-shaking, mind searing orgasm.

I lay next to her for a minute caressing her body while I caught my breath. *Where was I again? Who am I?* Then it all began to fade away. I took a quick shower and made some small talk with her as we dressed, and then we quietly returned alone, to our lives.

Tania Sucks Maddog

MADDOG

Well, Guadalupe pulled a no-show for her noon appointment with me at my room last Thursday and I wasn't pleased. I was extremely wounded from the debauchery of the night before and just really wanted to bust a nut. So after I wandered to the electronic store on Constitución (scolding Guadalupe on the way and rescheduling appointment for later) to get some cords for the VCR, I decided I needed a quick fix.

It's 2pm and I head out to find a SG to aid me in blowing a load. So off I go. Really all I was looking for was a nice, relaxing blowjob. I was way too tired and hungover to go through the motions of fucking. I hit Constitución and head towards Coahuila in search of the first attractive chica I could find. Well, it didn't take long.

As I cross Coahuila, I spot a fairly tall, attractive puta standing near the ice cream shop. This was Tania, about 5'10", past-her-shoulders black hair, thin legs with nice tight ass and nice C-cup titties. Very attractive facial features. She was wearing skin-tight blue jeans and a short sleeve tight black top. I'm thinking this will work so I walk up to her and start negotiating a deal. Tania's English is non-existent and my brain wasn't working on all cylinders so I just looked in her eyes and said, "Sucky, 20 dolares."

She looked back at me kind of confused so I said "Solamente

boca," and she seemed to understand my wishes. So off we go into that little dungeon of a motel that's right there.

Don't ask me the name of the place. I'm sure some of you know and I've passed it hundreds of times myself, but never really paid much attention. Maybe it's called the Hacienda. I don't know or care at this point. We walk up to the cashier where Tania asks me for $5 for the room. I give it to her. They hand over her supplies and a towel and she leads me back through the cave-like darkness into a room.

I asked Tania if she would let me take a picture of her, but she declined. I'm sure if I would have offered her a few bucks she would have let me, but I was too busy thinking about the this lovely creature sucking my cock and wanted to get the show on the road.

So Tania places a towel on the bed and motions me to lie down. I'm stripped down to my socks in an instant (white, not black this time) and am lying on my back in great anticipation. Tania removes her jeans and panties, exposing her beautiful tight ass and cute little bush, and joins me on the bed. I was a bit confused that she even removed her jeans in the first place being that I never mentioned anything about fucking her, but didn't mind the view. However, she did not remove her top, which I almost protested about, but I was just there for her to suck my dick so it really didn't make much of a difference. Let the games begin!

Tania begins to gently stroke my cock and play with my balls, which quickly produces the desired results of rock hard attention. I lie back and admire as she places the condom on my throbbing cock and begins to get to work. Tania's technique was good. She was a very energetic cocksucker. Lots of tongue action around my head with quite a bit of nut massaging.

At first, she was teasingly sucking me slow and gentle, but it wasn't long before her head was pistoning up and down in a frenzied sucking motion, engulfing as much of my manhood as she could get in her mouth. She made sure that her hair was pulled to the side so that I could enjoy watching her in action and occasionally I would run my hands through her hair guiding her head up and down as she sucked my swollen cock. Every once in a while, I would thrust my cock up deeper into her mouth and I could see her discomfort as she seemed to want to gag as the head pushed into the back of her throat. So I let up and let her do her work. And work she did!

It was very nice. She continued to suck for a good ten minutes before she finally came up air with a look of *please-cum-soon* on her face.

I could see that her mouth was getting tired and suggested that she jump on top if she'd prefer and ride the snake. She said, "Sexo?" and I nodded, but she then said that this would be an additional fee.

I said no and instructed her to get back to sucking my dick. She complied and really began to vigorously massage my balls in some attempt to milk the cum out of them while continuing to suck away. This went on for another heavenly five minutes and even though I could feel some twinges of an oncoming orgasm, I could see that she was getting exhausted and decided to cut her a break.

I told her to finish me off with her manos sin condom and she gladly accepted the invitation. With one hand, she continued to rub my balls and with the other she began to stroke me good and hard. I laid back and closed my eyes and she pumped my love muscle. Within minutes, I knew that I was about to blow.

Sure enough, I blew my love juice while she continued to pump me dry. I was spent and she grabbed some toilet paper and cleaned me off, leaving extra for me to finish the job while she went to the bathroom to wash her hands.

I got up and dressed and thanked her for her efforts by giving her a small kiss on the cheek. We exited together and I winked and smiled at her as I headed back onto Constitución completely satisfied. My only complaint was that she did not remove her top and would reposition herself when I would try to play with her tits while she was sucking me.

I know I overpaid, but it was worth it to me. I ran into a few Amigos while walking back to the Leyva and one confirmed that Tania had been the SG that he's been fucking himself recently. Everything for $20, I might add, with a $5 tip.

Next time I'll get my money's worth out of her, but today, I was happy with her performance and the end results. Overall a successful mission and one that held me over until Guadalupe showed up at my room a few hours later.

Stay Flexible

DOH

This is my once-a-year trip that I have been planning for a LONG time. I was packed and loaded and ready to go. I had my Vitamin V, disposable camera, condoms and I'd saved up the love juice for a week+.

But if you don't want to read a long report, I'll go ahead and give you:

The Short Version

- BBBJ with club girl at Beverly Hills.
- Shitty fuck at Mermaids.
- BJ with another club girl at Beverly Hills.
- Go home with no wait at the border.

For those who want all the details of this adventure, settle in for:

The Long Version
My Original Plan

- Warm up at a Revo strip club.
- Go to Zona and get to Mermaids to find a cutie or two in a schoolgirl outfit and bang the hell out of them with a package price.
- Go back across the border, grinning my ass off.

WHAT ACTUALLY HAPPENED
- Plan falls apart.
- Spent more money than planned in order to make myself feel a little better.
- Found a diamond in the rough.
- Went back across border to US with a smirk.

THE DETAILS

Finally made the trip across the border with two friends on Monday at 7:30pm. Took a taxi (the yellow ones, yeah, I know, but it wasn't that bad). Requested to go to Beverly Hills and he let us off close on the corner with Revolución. Turns out that Revo was completely torn up and no cars were getting through. Jackhammers were running all over the place and you had to be careful not to trip on any holes while crossing the street.

The first place my two friends and I went was Beverly Hills. It was empty. This didn't look good, but I figured we'd try it out for a couple of minutes. Got mineral water and sat away from the stage. I sat between my friends and the waiters brought three girls to us, two of which sat next to my friends, but the one for me (who had a smoking spinner body) decided that since I didn't want a lap dance within the first three seconds of sitting down she didn't want to sit on my lap and she took off.

Her loss since I would have had once if she wasn't such a bitch about it. Got the usual pitch from the waiters for a $40 BJ. Turned that down, too. I'll play when I feel ready for it.

My friend Jake had an older 40-ish (her face looked it) bleach blonde with fake tits, which were pretty hard. My other friend Jim had a 30-ish sandy blonde, who wasn't much to look at and unfortunately wore a weird black-and-white striped outfit which made her look really lumpy and fat, although I found out later that her body wasn't that bad. But that outfit just HAD to go.

They were friendly enough and stayed with my friends even

though they didn't buy them drinks and didn't get lap dances from them. I didn't mind that no one sat with me as I could just enjoy the dancer on stage.

Jake soon wanted to go sit next to the stage and the blonde (Diana from Rosarito) followed him over to sit next to him. They spoke a while and she started getting a little touchy feely as I was busy giving tips to the dancer and getting some tits rubbed in my face with an occasional stick shift. All of a sudden, Diana sits next to me after Jake said to go to me with a shit-eating grin. That was okay since I didn't figure I'd do much with an older woman because that wasn't in my game plan.

And here's where the plan gets messed up.

Diana starts talking to me and I'm replying in my three-years-of-high-school-Spanish and she says that everyone's really friendly in TJ, blah-blah-blah. Then she asks if I want a BJ or sex.

I lie to her and say that I have a GF and that she'd know if I banged anyone. She said she understood and asked if I wanted a BJ. I hemmed and hawed with the Bill Clinton line that even if a BJ wasn't sex, I wasn't sure. (Since I was planning to save my money for the MP.)

So we continue to talk about other things and then she lets me pet her kitty and when I did that, she proceeded to jam my finger up her. *Okay!* Now my interest is starting to get peaked. She also begins to stick shift me on a constant basis while we're still talking and even though I'm watching the show, having Little Doh stroked is really getting to me. She asks if I want a lap dance and Little Doh reaches into my pocket and gets a $20 out and gives it to her before Brain gets to even think about it.

When we get in the booth, without asking, she unzips me, pulls open my pants and shorts, and gives me a couple of sucks before she sits on me and rubs Little Doh back and forth on her pussy. This goes on for two or three songs. At the end of the dance, she asks if I want a BJ for $50. Brain comes back and says the sure-fire thing to kill the deal: "I don't like blowjobs with a condom."

"Okay. No condom," she says.

Well, WTF do I do now? I say, "Okay."

We go to the back room and I give the waiter $50. He tries to sell me a condom, but I say I have them already.

Diana closes the curtain and off comes the pants and shorts and she begins the most awesome, wet, sloppy BBBJ I've ever had. Technique was awesome and I had to think about baseball scores, eating dirt, having to take out the garbage when I got home, anything to keep from popping. (See, I still wanted to do the MP fantasy but this was really fucking things up.)

She almost took me over the top, but Brain prevailed and we stopped after fifteen minutes and left with smiles on both of our faces. She said if the waiter asked just to tell him I had used a condom. She left the club soon after. Jake had realized what a freaky girl she was and he knew I would enjoy her. He didn't partake because he actually has morals and a GF that he's faithful to. I respect that, but I like pussy more.

We walk around to Pussycats and it was dead. No one in there. Walk out and head to Peanuts & Beer, which was worse.

After we get in there, no one is dancing and it's dead. The waiter didn't even try to get us to stay because he knew it was stupid to even try. We leave and head to La Zona. Walk down Articulo 123, down Niños Heroes, and then on to Coahuila. Tons of SGs, some with very nice legs.

Remember how I said I can't ever get any SGs to call out to me? I must have some kind of natural SG repellent on 'cuz the same thing happened to me on this trip, too. My friends got the "Sssst" and got their shirts tugged, but not me.

I was thinking of asking some of them just to take nekkid pictures, but I didn't have the nerve.

We walk into HK and the music was WAY too fucking loud. The girls all looked bored and no one was looking very attractive.

Had to get out before our eardrums broke. The doorman said that the lesbian show started in two hours It was 9pm. We left.

Went to Mermaids. Dead. No one in there. One pudgy girl was outside and when we went inside, she ran past us to start dancing on the empty stage. Not a good way to start. No other girls that I could see in the club. We left.

Now I started to think that my plan was stupid and I should have banged Diana. We go to CC and there were several folks in there, but nothing interesting in terms of chicas. So we eat at Al Capone's, which was really good.

Head back to HK for the show and actually ducked into Miami since the music wasn't as loud there and we could see if the show started through the glass windows. Waited there for an hour and no show. Fuckers.

We left again and went back to Mermaids. Still no clients there but more girls now. Most were a little pudgy. Waiter tells me they had called the girls from the other MP to come down. We wait. Guy tries to give me the $40 massage price. I turn him down repeatedly. Finally, some other girls in street clothes come down and with some desperation sinking in, I pick Elizabeth (5'0, blonde, looked slim in black clothing). Ask for the package price from the mesero and he quotes $100.

I pick room #5, because it's the only one with a shower and the mesero said she'd shower with me in there.

Wrong.

First thing is when we go upstairs, she heads to a room near the street. Mesero tells her it's the shower room and she has a little annoyed look going. We get to the room, she finds out it's a package price and she's even more annoyed. I should have bailed but the tuff guy broke and I wanted a trophy fuck now. I strip down and she starts to do the same. Then I see out her tits are a little droopy and her thighs and tummy were hidden by the clothes.

I shower by myself.

Get a basic rub down while she's in her panties. No talking, no good vibes at all. She gives a pathetic, lackluster BJ, which lasts one minute and I start to worry about getting it up. There's nothing like feeling like shit and trying to fuck. She forces it in and nothing is happening so she gets up and tries a hand job with an occasional suck. I'm busy concentrating on the idea that I just blew $100 so I resort to thinking about my MILF co-worker to get it up and that works. She gets on and I just shoot my wad and I'm done. It's over quick 'cuz I didn't want to prolong this. I take a shower. She takes a shower. And that's it.

Finally, I find my really bored friends and Jake wants to go back to a strip club, so we walk to Beverly Hills again. Couple of cuties sit on my friends' laps and I start tipping the dancer who I find out is Myra. (5'5", 130, nice body, natural B's.)

I want to leave TJ with a good feeling so I agree to a BJ. I knew I just popped so I played hard to get by saying a BBBJ or nothing. Myra and the waitress go back in forth in Spanish and I know she doesn't want to do it that way. But finally she agrees after the waitress says something that I can't hear.

It's $50, but I only have twenties so she says, "Okay, it's $50 and $10 for the room." It's really late now, so I don't bother arguing. First thing that happens is my pants come down and like lightning, she's slipping on a condom and sucking rapidly. Now I didn't really expect a BBBJ, but you never know what you'll get if you don't ask. She's pretty good and she's trying to get me off, but I just can't come a second time in fifteen minutes. This was my grudge BJ and she worked it for fifteen minutes and had to stop.

I felt bad for her 'cuz I knew I wasn't going to pop, but this was for me. As soon as she stopped, she asked, "Okay?"

I said yes, and she just leaves me sitting in the booth with my pants around my ankles alone. I zip up and grab my friends and we leave. Got a yellow cab to drop us off at the border and walk without incident to the US. Thirty-second wait and we're through.

The second BJ helped me feel better about the MP. But I should have gone with my gut and went for Diana who would have been much more fun and had a lot of personality.

Oh well. Next time.

Lunchtime Mission

CRAIGFROMSD

Man, I was really wanting some Mexican food for lunch today. Not Taco Bell, I'm talking 'bout real Mexican food. I knew that an Adelberto's wouldn't do it. I needed some place with excitement. I needed a place where the sever doesn't know any English and I don't know the language that they're speaking. I needed the opportunity to drink a Fanta or a Coca Cola Light. I needed to eat something that makes me think, "This might not be a good idea." I needed Tijuana and I needed a food cart.

Oh, and I needed to drain a few ounces of jizz from my cock as well.

At 1pm the decision was made and the car was headed south. Fifteen minutes later, I was pulling into the parking lot across from Jack in the Box. I prefer this one during the day as it's a very short walk back to the car and I make one right turn and I'm on the 805 going north. I did a quick change of shirts in the car and started towards the border. Decided to walk the entire way to Zona Norte as it was beautiful today. However, as I felt the sweat dripping off my nuts as I walked across the bridge over the empty riverbed, I considered that walking all the way might have been a bad idea. Regardless, I soldiered on and by 2:15pm, I had eased in to the cool darkness of Adelita.

I was slightly impressed with the selection and a little taken aback by the semi-large crowd that was there. Ordered a mineral water and took a seat at the front bar.

Within minutes, the first potential chica comes up. Her name was Blue. Nice body, tall at 5'8"+. I was sitting down. Smaller up top. Slightly flirty. Probably would have been a little more interested if she wasn't the first girl up to the base. She sat on my lap for a while and offered her wares: $60 basic deal. She kept trying to feed me Ruffles potato chips that were covered in salsa. *Uhhh, no thanks.* I wouldn't say I was getting a bad vibe from her, but she wasn't really impressing me. Said that she has worked there for a year. Somebody has got to know the info on her. Maybe next round.

Then I saw this top-heavy chica looking at me. I'm thinking, "She is digging me. I should offer to buy her a drink."

Then I remembered where I was. I was in a fucking brothel and I should see if she will let me stick it in her ass for $25.

Her name is Alexandria. She's from Guadalajara. Real jugs. 20 years old. Cute face. Heavy up top (D's), small everywhere else. Nice pink top. Great English. Me likey, likey. $60 to go upstairs, standard deal. "Yeah, let's go. But I want to cum on your tits."

In the room, she started in on one of the best CBJs that I've ever gotten. Well, I'll say it now. The best covered blowjob I've ever received. Fantastic. I didn't think I would ever be able to bust a CBJ nut, but I came (*get it?*) pretty close.

Stuck it in her for about six thrusts, pulled out, and proceeded to strafe her tits with my man chowder. I think she thought I would have forgotten about cumming on her tits, but I didn't. Don't worry if you were next. She took a nice shower and cleaned herself up afterwards.

No knock as I only took about 20 minutes total.

I went back downstairs, made a phone call, and walked over to the alley to get a few tacos. Had some decent carne asada tacos and a Coca Cola Light and considered calling it a nice productive lunch. But then I thought I better head back to Adelita for one last walk through. It had been a while for me since I'd gone down south so I figured, *Why the hell not?*

I went back in and stood in the back for a bit. Took a seat at the back bar and up walks Jessica from Mazatlan or Acapulco (can't remember which). Decent face, but not exactly my body type. In fact, her body was a bit of a turn off. But then she came up with a great deal. Massage, BJ, fucky, and she would let me drop the baby batter in her mouth… all for $30. She showed me her jello-y tits and I thought, *WWJD?*

In the room, she asks me if I'm clean. Oh God. Sure. But she still wants to wash my dick. I'm thinking, "Honey, were you walking behind me on the pedestrian bridge and smelling my stank nuts?" I told her that it was probably a good idea because those stinky nuts are going to be banged against her nose.

She asked if I wanted a cover for the BJ. "Yeah, probably a good idea," I reply. Lame blowjob.

She wants me to fuck her and I'm thinking that it won't work. Instead I tell her to give me one hell of a handjob. Well, she did. She worked magic. That jizz harvester yanked and pulled like she was shucking an ear of corn. I got on top of her and I finished off on her face. She really appreciated that.

Out the door and to a cab. Twenty minute linea. Hit my car at 4pm. Back in the office by 4:20.

Great day.

AMIGO COMMENTARY

DickArmy: Why bother to go back to the office? You were probably in a daze anyway, or at least in need of a nappie.

CraigfromSD: I went back because I knew I could look everyone in the eye and think to myself, "You didn't let your trouser snake vomit on a chick's face today."

Experiment in Madness

Paco

Yesterday I felt like going to TJ and I had been thinking about trying an experiment on myself to delay ejaculation; in other words, to last longer before I cum. My quack doctor a few months back gave me samples of Paxil CR because I told him I had anxiety at times. I read about the pills, and the pills are really for depression, obsessive-compulsive disorders, and panic attacks. But a few doctors prescribe them for premature ejaculation.

I was watching the Lakers lose yesterday and feeling depressed, so what the hell. I'm going to take a Paxil before I have to throw them all away. I was a little scared because it fucks with your serotonin levels, but as soon as I took them a calm came over me, a surreal feeling. I was feeling a little light-headed, too, so I went to my bed and watched the game. I no longer cared what was happening in the game.

I was feeling better, but it was still too early to get to TJ, so I stopped by a casino to play blackjack. I wanted to make a few extra bucks because I was starting to lose money on the few penny stocks I owned. I feel you have better odds in a casino playing blackjack using basic strategy than buying penny stocks. Besides, I also know how to count cards.

Well, I didn't make out too well at the casino, but only lost about $250 before continuing on my journey to TJ.

Finally, I got to TJ, but I needed some Viagra to go with the Paxil, so I stopped off and bought some from a 24-hour pharmacy near First and Revolución. Then I went to Hong Kong and got a beer to wash down the Viagra. With the complete cocktail of Paxil, Viagra, and liquor, I was feeling great. The Paxil was making me happy, along with the fine pussy on stage. I was almost ready to find me a lady to complete the experiment but then I was starting to have weird thoughts. I kept thinking that I was David Banner from the Hulk, and that I was going to freak out.

As this was happening, I could not find a bargirl I wanted to try to have extended sex with. My favorites were not there. I wandered hopelessly bar to bar looking for possible GFE girls, but I wasn't sure whom to pick. There were plenty of trophy fucks, but I was after something else.

Finally, I ended up where I started. I went upstairs in Hong Kong and there was a nice girl with curly hair, with a black dress on that had a slit up the side. Her name? I still don't know even asking three times. She was about 5'4", 105, cute. She says she is 26. Her face looks older.

I brought her a drink, and we settle on $50. She doesn't do BJs, but does DFK. I was tired of looking so I said, "Let's go."

We get up to the room, and she gives me the condom. I tell her I don't really like condoms, and I would give her an extra ten bucks if we don't use it. She said okay. (The Paxil was doing the talking; I always wear a condom for sexo.) Anyway, she lifts up her dress and slides down on my dick. Oh, it felt so good without the condom, but I asked her, "What's with the dress? Take it off, please."

She took it off and removed her padded bra. She had little tits, small A's. Matter of fact, I realized I'd never seen such small tits while she was going up and down.

After 20 minutes of cowgirl and reverse cowgirl, we got in the mish position, with good DFK kissing, and pounding away with my uncovered shaft.

After 10 minutes of fucking like this, I could not hold back anymore, my jizz shot all over inside her pussy. *Uh-oh.* She told me I could fuck her without a condom, but to please take my dick out before I cum.

Oh well, I'm sure my sperm enjoyed the journey in the pussy. (I was having weird thoughts again. I saw a Discovery show a few months back that said throughout history women do cheat on men, and sperm has evolved to create defensive sperm to fight others guys' sperm. I was picturing my sperm fighting other sperm.)

After I came, I took my dick out. It smelled of pussy. I looked closer at this girl, and said I made a mistake doing her sin condom. She was a little pissed I came in her.

We both raced to the shower, her to wash out the sperm that was oozing out of her pussy, and me to clean my dick as best I can. I can't afford to catch anything. I couldn't piss, so I said goodbye, and went to AB to buy a beer, so I could piss as soon as possible, to wash out anything.

The experiment was over. Because I went sin condom I was unable to last over half an hour, and after being with this chica, I didn't feel like finding anyone else that night.

I just went home, took off my pants and noticed my dick still had pussy smell on it, so I took another shower. I also took a big antibiotic to kill any possible STD. Yah, I know bad idea, but my quack doctor has told me that it will kill most problems.

Final thoughts? Maybe I'll have a few later. I still have a headache; that fucking Paxil is still working.

Code Name: Crying Game

C-DIDDY

Military slang for bloody military operations is known as Wetworks. Up until this point, I'd heard of it but never experienced it. This mission is being filed under 2004.01.21 but shall be remembered as Operation Crying Game. This sting operation was completed in the record time of two hours flat. A personal record, but at costs that still remain to be seen.

2nd Decontamination

I made it safely home from TJ by 6pm for decontamination protocol. I jumped in the shower and first let the hot water wash me down for several minutes then scrubbed myself down. I then lathered myself with Dial antibacterial soap. After drying off, I soaked my genitals with isopropyl alcohol crying "Oh gawd!" under my breath as I tried to cleanse myself via mind and body.

Just 20 minutes earlier, I was crossing into US territory as a second border agent interrogated me. "Why was I in Mexico? Where was I headed to? Where did I go? Where was I born?" The border agent was reading my eyes, trying to detect an accent or whether my eyes or body language told of any lies. She intercepted me toward the exit after the first border guard let me pass as we chuckled how my photo ID featuring a hairstyle taken seven years ago made me look like the artist formerly known as Prince. She gave up her little tough act since this operative wasn't compromising a thing about the Zone.

Disgusting Salsa

Walking back to the border at dusk was good exercise for the six tacos I had downed. I couldn't help thinking about the color red. I poured red salsa over my chips as a few drops splattered to the ground, like blood. As always, the six tacos were excellent, but seeing the salsa pour into the taco crevice just sickened me. *How could I be eating after what I had just seen?* Whatever the case, this fugitive was thankful that I made it that far without Federales on my trail halfway back to what the natives call "La Linea." As I saw my hands dripping in red salsa, I regressed once more to a half hour earlier.

Wetworks

As I patted down my crotch with a paper towel, the hint of pink on the toilet paper indicated that there was fluid contact with the bottom region of my staff. I got up and carefully peeled off the condom then ran to the sink to wash myself off. Thankfully, I had my Band-Aid® antiseptic foam and just sprayed it on liberally and just let it soak instead of dying it off. I had held in my piss for an hour before visiting the alley and hopefully that flushed out any possible remnants that may have reached my urethra. I handed the petite puta 300 pesos and told her to beat it.

It was only moments earlier that she just took off her bottoms and walked to bed with her runway model body. Her blowjob technique started out with her sucking the top edge while rubbing my staff with her hand. After a minute of this nonsense, I thought it was time to press the issue at hand, literally. I grabbed a handful of her hair and pushed her head down as my staff disappeared in her mouth.

I expected some resistance from this forceful intervention but she just went with the flow. I admit that the chauvinistic nature of it all was a real turn on as I dribbled her head like a basketball.

As we moved in to missionary, I felt like an old pervert determining whether this housekeeper deserved her raise while the wife was out. Her pussy hair was naturally trim. It didn't look shaved nor like a bush. I was enjoying the housekeeper fantasy up until the time I withdrew and wanted to change positions. Alarmingly, I looked down and my condom was blood soaked. She was working during her period. *Would I retreat or finish this bitch off?* I stuck my prick back in and kept pumping rounds into her a few minutes more until climax. By then, we were a bloody mess. If I were going to jail, I at least got one final climax.

Paranoia

I've been scouting this young spinner for the past several weeks. Her name is Cindy from Veracruz. She looks very Spanish with a skinny petite frame standing around 5'2" with brown curly hair flowing a little past her shoulders. She stands about ten feet west of the Hong Kong entrance and uses the Cascadas Hotel. She'd probably sell more if she reduced the size of her Italian-like nose.

On previous occasions, she always got my juices flowing by wearing tight jeans that formed a camel toe in her crotch. She's consistently said she's 20 years old, but I've always had my doubts since she looked barely 18. After passing her by her for several weeks, I figured that TJ's finest would have put her in a paddy wagon by now if she didn't have the proper credentials.

Still, I made sure the alley was clear of uniformed officers before approaching her.

I was also paranoid walking with her to the hotel making sure no cops were rounding the corner or standing across the street. A hard knock on a nearby room had me wondering if the policia were searching for me. *Did they have the wrong hotel room?* I took a peek out the blinds but it was the towel boy doing his rounds cleaning a nearby room. *What the heck was I doing there? Was it the giant TJ arch vagina that had me wriggling toward it like a little sperm?*

TOUCH AND GO

Yes, it was the Cialis in me from the previous day that drove me toward TJ's aluminum arch after work. I crossed the border at 4pm and wondered how fast I could get laid and be back home. This, I thought, could be a quick and easy mission for the record books.

TJ Hookers: This Is Their Scam

Various

TJ Lord: Well, my buddy Rick, who I introduced to La Zona not too long ago, had a bad experience after I took him down a couple of times. He wanted to continue going even on the times that I couldn't make it down there with him but he is not experienced enough. Yet he decided to go "Lone Ranger" while he was still in training. And even though he had already gone through my TJ Safety Class 101, along with many other classes, something bad happened to him.

He arrived at La Zona around 9:30pm and wandered around between AB and CC drinking some beer until he found the right material. He took a chica upstairs from AB around 11pm. From there, he continued drinking until about 1am and then headed back to his hotel, which was roughly two miles away from La Zona.

But around 3am, Steve decides to go back to La Zona because he felt like having a BBBJ, so he picked up a chica in the alley and convinced her $$$ to go with him to his hotel for the BBBJ. They went back to his hotel, the chica gave him a BBBJ and after that, she left in a taxi.

He says he was always awake and on his five senses. Also, according to him, he never took his eyesight from her, yet in the morning, he realized that he was missing all of his puta money left from his wallet ($580), which was inside of a zippered pocket inside his jacket. Regardless, he was still pleased with the trip and with the experience despite the fact of this "incident".

So be careful when you take 'em to your rooms. When you do it, you have to make sure that you do it with one of your regular chicas that you have already done a few times. I'm still going to go back with my friend Steve to ID the puta (if we see her again). Be safe out there!

Juanster: Along the same vein, I had a somewhat embarrassing incident occur to me about six months ago. Humiliating, because I consider myself a seasoned monger who should have known better. I lodged in the Hotel Tapatio located on the next street following the main thoroughfare; a quaint, pseudo dive that offers porn and SKY channels.

Now I have been given the heads-up by many chicas that this place has a "reputation", much like what the Hotel Leyva had in the late 90s until the heat fell on it. Always the rebel, I scoffed at their warnings and bunked up in a room anyway. To my delight, I found that a good crop of chicas did their R&R here as well. Before long, I had three chicas in my room with beer and the pervasive kriko fogging up the room. The beer was being served in plastic cups; that was my last recollection for that moment. I woke up ten hours later without my wallet and its $800.

Avisado: There appears to be a weakness inherent in the male psychology, which reads something like this:

"Gee, she must really like me 'cause she lets me fuck her every week. What's more, we spent the entire night together on Tuesday and went shopping on Wednesday. She must really dig me big time."

Guys believe that just because a chica spends time with them that there is something really there. Chicas, on the other hand, can remain very detached while appearing to be emotionally present.

Weaker sex? That is debatable.

Easy: Fellas, my concern for my Amigo is in HIS words: "My situation is very different. She really loves me and I'm too intelligent to get scammed."

How many times and how many different hombres have gone down this road?

Every one of us has believed our relationship is different. She's different. We're different. We're gonna make it. Together. All I gotta do is keep throwing $$$$$$$$$$$$$$$$$$$$$$$ at her and she'll change. She doesn't want to work as a puta, she told me so. She's told me a hundred times, "I lub you too much, papi!" And I lubba her. She'll never go back to the club. She'll never have a real Mexican BF.

My Amigo is a very intelligent hombre. I know this for a fact. But it has NOTHING to do with an hombre's intelligence. It's about ILLUSION. Chicas know exactly how to keep us feeding on the illusion week after week, cumming back to them. And to only them.

In reality, we are kinda like the chica's employer; they need us for the lifestyle, the support, the money, but they hate us. They smile every time we show up, but inside, they're thinking, "Okay, get that smile on! Here we go again."

Then when we leave, they call their real Mex BF and tell heem, "Cum home, baby, hee's gone." And they take the money we've given them—money for rent, utilities, groceries, clothes, etc—and go spend it on/with their Mex BFs. Or they head back into the club we found them in, thinking we'll never know, and pass out their phone number and collect other hombres' phone numbers, and get ready for the day we get bored with them. 'Cause they know we will. After all, how much trust can/will a puta have in an hombre she met in a whore bar? NONE.

Paying for plastic or lipo is ridiculous. Paying to keep a puta out of the business is even more ridiculous. Living The Illusion is nonsense. I speak from experience. Once was enough for me.

Willie: Had a chica pull up in a taxi, quiz the clerk as to what room I was staying in, and she pounded on my door until I opened it. I was talking on my cell at the time she burst into the room. When she grabbed the phone and heard a girl's voice, she threw my cell across the room and gave me a nice right hook. Needless to say, the sex was hot 'n heavy that night. But the next morning, I got outta dodge.

Sampson: I had this novia situation with a chica from La Tropa a couple of years ago. I wasn't that in to her, but she never charged and so I saw her quite a bit. She had a network of guys that would let her know if they saw me in town, and she would come look for me in all the bars. She actually found me in Adelita one day. I wasn't too threatened by it, and I actually thought it was somewhat funny. I remember getting pissed at her at one night in La Tropa, and I grabbed a new chica and said to her, "Look, I have a girlfriend over there, and I'm pissed at her. Do you want to go home with me and fuck tonight? It is only for one night." She and I had a really fun time, and the novia was very apologetic the next day.

Eventually she crossed the border and moved to Orange County. I had met her uncles and family, but soon separated myself from the situation.

Also had this chica from Las Chavelas that I referred to as "Not So Hot". She used to go to La Tropa to look for me sometimes. I often thought of moving her in with me, but I don't think she could make enough money.

One night I was out with an Amigo while my chica was on vacation so we are partying at Bar Charlie's where he hooks up with a cute little tenderonie and asks if he can use my apartment. I give him the key and I go to fuck around in Zona Norte. I walk into Las Chavelas around 5am and see a friend of "Not So Hot". The friend tells me not to leave, that she will go get her (she lived in Cascadas). I tell her not to bother, but minutes later there is "Not So Hot" carrying an overnight case. I tell her that she can't come home with me because my apartment is occupied. *No problemo!* She drags me upstairs to her room where I find my picture plastered all over her walls. Mind you, not one picture of another man in there... pretty fricking intimidating.

BorderSushi: As demonstrated by the mongers... another beauty of the ZN is that even if you have a psychotic bitch chasing you down, the wonderful border keeps us men from the psycoticas separated. I've been busy the past few days trying to gently shake loose a chica that I met recently here in the States. I let this babe suck my cock a few times; my jizz must be tainted with opium because she's constantly calling me for more. I sensed something strange from our conversations... intangible, but I have a feeling she could cause trouble if I give her a severe cut off. Possibly the type that would pull a "Kobe Bryant" thing on my sorry ass. Be grateful for the ZN chicas!

DosEquis: There I was in the Zona, gathering my thoughts, my senses, my nuts, my reserves, and everything else that gets depleted in a 24-hour TJ adventure. As I am about to head home, I run into a favorita. My favorita tells me, "Ooooo, DosEquis, quiero hacer amor contigo... muy, muy sabrosa."

"Ehhhhhh, mi amor, gotta go, no puedo!"

Actually, my left nutsack had perhaps 1/1000 of a gram of nut juice left inside, but I was in no mood for sex due to the last night's experience with two putas.

As I tried to pull away from her, she leans into me, saddles me, sticks her tongue down my mouth, exposes a nipple out of her shirt, and lets my tongue lick her nipple free of charge... or so I thought. She then says since I'm leaving and don't have time to bang her, could she borrow $20 from me?

"Borrow?" I thought, "Ohhhhhhhhh, sure!"

But without thinking further, I was pulling out my wallet handing her a 20-dollar bill. *What the hell did I do that for?*

Shit, it was her "puta power" that got a hold of my senses! Shit, fuck, piss, suck, mofo, tits, damn. *I was putawinked!* A kiss goodbye and I was off to the sunset to cross the border negative 20 dollars.

Moral of story, be careful! These putas know how to work their magic spell. Yet, to be honest, it was all worth it.

Puta Power: 1; Will Power: 0.

You all have been warned.

Pastor G Spot: Sounds like you got fucked for twenty. Not bad, really. You saved the room fee. I can usually say no to a girl until she pulls down her bra, grabs the back of my head, pulls down on it with one hand, unzips me with the other, grabs my Johnson, and thumbs the head. Puta wants the money fronted? Who can say no?

How I Spent $400 and Got No Sex

Mad Ogre

Yes, I think I am the stupidest PLM of all time. The first night was fantastic. I bought her drinks for a couple of hours, took her upstairs, and had some of the best sex ever in the zone. Second night a week later, I took her up to the VIP room twice, great sex. Second time in the VIP room I promised her $80 but after paying el mesero por las cervezas I didn't have the $80 for her, so I left her there at 4am and told her I'd be back next week.

Next week rolls around and it was the third time with her. Maybe she was mad and I guess she got her revenge. I take her to La Perla restaurant at the beginning of her shift, then I ask her if I can spend the night at her house that night. She says yes.

My friend leaves us to get his own hotel room and asks her again and she tells him, "Sure, he can stay with me." So I buy her $7 beers all night long, her entire shift. From 7pm until 4am. I asked her several times to go upstairs with me, but she says just wait until after work then I can have her all night at her place. I even paid her back the $80 from the previous week, took her outside a couple times for tacos, etc, etc.

In total, I spent over $400 that night on her while she was at work. No sex. Around 4am, I say, "Vamos a tu casa."

She says, "Okay. Let me change my clothes and my tickets." She disappears in to the changing room for over an hour. I ask a mesero to check on her. He says she is almost ready.

But then, out she runs from the room and out of the front of the bar, across the street, and up into her hotel room. I am chasing behind, calling her name the whole time. The hotel manager stopped me from going up the stairs after her. She left me in the middle of TJ at 5am without a room to stay in.

So am I am the stupidest PLM of all time?

Is this a Guinness Book World Record for most money spent on a hooker without having any sex with her?

Is this the most pathetic story on here?

And the worst part is I went back to her two weeks later, blew another $180 on drinks, but at least I got her to come to my hotel for three hours of great sex this time. But when we got back to the bar, I had to "pagar la salida," which was $90 for three hours outside of Chavelas. Is that a real thing or another scam? Having to pay the bar for taking the girl out?

Now she wants me to drive the hijo de la nana to LA and find him a job so he doesn't go to jail for running with his hoodlum friends in TJ. Oh yeah, she says I can live with her in TJ if I want.

So am I el gran pendejo gringo en todo el mundo?

Is this the very definition of being a PLM?

At least I didn't send her any money for getting el hijo out of jail like she asked.

Amigo Commentary

BigDick: When I saw the title of this thread I thought it was going to be about me and my Filipina ex-gf. The part of your story that troubles me is you're resuming with her after she gave you the slip to return to her palatial hotel room. Of course, the changing room disappearing act is a basic move in the chica playbook, which they all read on the bus up from rural May-he-co wherein they transform from sweet farm girl to vixen puta.

SecretAsianMan: Please tell me you were smoking something other than cigarettes!

Creasy: BTW, I saw her thread on here and she's 150-peso SG quality. I'm being generous, too.

MelonBag: La Perla? What is it with all of you guys and your fetish for watching hookers shovel food in their mouths? They talk to you and you'll see pieces of cilantro stuck in their teeth. Yecch! And losers like Hornitos will buy a couple of fat chicks a half dozen hot dogs and that is the highlight of his night.

I don't understand why you guys can't just fuck the putas and treat them like the cum dumpsters they are supposed to be. Why try to treat them like dates? You'll just get in trouble with PLM tendencies. Outside of that, I enjoyed the original post in this thread.

Divest: I'm surprised you had the courage to post your embarrassing story… Well, courage or shamelessness, I don't know.

Asshole: It happens. You are not the first—nor the last—monger to get ficha fucked. As a matter of fact, it sounds like a typical night out for Horny-toes. All it cost you was $400, but you can survive that. I suggest drinking and fucking as many girls in the same bar as possible. That way she knows how much money she lost. It will make the $400 look like chump change.

Rancheroi: Hey, don't feel bad, Amigo. I would venture to say that almost any guy who has chased panocha in the zone has gotten scammed in one form or another, and you will have all kinds of advice thrown at you on how to avoid it, but the simple fact is, you are an adult, it is your money, so do as you see fit.

Of anything that I have learned in the zone, is ANY act of kindness towards locals by an outsider is usually looked upon as a sign of weakness, and you will get sized up pretty quick for a bigger take-off of funds by either deception or a bait and switch.

As far as buying girls drinks in the bars, I understand that they have to sell drinks to make their money, but their terms of employment with the club is not my problem. I am the customer and I set the rules on how I roll in the zone, not her, and especially not some drug cartel assholes who happen to own the zone club that I may be in at the time.

It is very seldom that I ever buy a BG a drink in the club, mostly because I don't drink. Why would I buy her a drink to make small talk which is near impossible over the blast of music in the club? Instead, I could be upstairs jamming my dick in her ass having a better time rather than watching her drink on my dime.

I would suggest that you lay off the BGs for a while and investigate the SG scene, since if you know the game around the zone, you can have some great times for a fraction of the price, and at times with SGs, you also have a choice of which hotel that you want to use, rather than with the BGs where you gotta use their overpriced rooms along with all the cumboys' bullshit early knocking.

But I do appreciate your written account of what happened, since I'm sure it will enlighten some new monger in the future on his first few trips to the zone of what could happen to him if he plays "Mr. Nice Guy" to the BG sharks that are waiting amongst the shadows for him.

In time you may become a cynical, selfish, uncaring, cheap-ass, fuck-her-first-then-pay-her-after, loudmouthed, demanding, intolerant prick like me, and you will no longer be concerned about what a Zona puta wants or doesn't want, just as long as YOU get what you want, because YOU are all that matters in the grand scheme of things.

Asshole: True words. The Zona is a shark tank, and you are the chum.

I am always amazed that small acts of kindness, or acts of compassion, are construed in such a negative light in the Zona. Your American sense of fair play needs to be left at the border. In the Zona, you take or you are taken.

If I come out with a decent session or two for a decent price, I am thrilled. Even after years in the Zona, I make mistakes that cost me. Usually small amounts, but I still get taken on occasion. It reminds me to be on my toes, so that I don't fall victim to a larger scam.

Sonero: The Zona is a unique environment. It is about as close as you can get to being in a prison without being in one (some will debate this!). Many of these guys are fresh out of Cali prisons. I think a lot of the same rules apply in the Zona as in prison. I agree with watching your back and taking care of you and yours but I don't necessarily see compassion as weakness. I think the word "respect" will take you a long way in the Zona. Respect for yourself and for the other person. Meaning be strong, but also don't disrespect. It's not an easy thing to do if you feel threatened.

I haven't been in prison (thank God) but I do know some of those street guys. I know them because I am on their streets! I will from time to time buy a taco for somebody who is hungry or give out cigs (dirt cheap). I would appreciate that if I was on the streets.

The situation in the Zona is fragile. That is what makes it exciting.

The Goal

NINJA23

When I first arrived, I walked a couple of laps and checked out all the SGs and the major bars. HK had a fantastic selection. Adelita was pretty damn good, too. Chicago Club was downright scary; I would not have fucked a single girl in there, even for free (my leche is very important to conserve!) Tropical was okay, but nothing really caught my eye. Went to other places like Play Boy—OMG train wreck, but not as bad as Chicago Club.

There were three SGs in the alley that I was very attracted to. However, only two that I could fuck because one of them I have on freeze. The three girls I was attracted to:

Sol @ Michoacán: I'm trying to develop a program on her so I'm not fucking her for a month so that rules one out.

Number 2 was Daniella @ The Mini, super cute but with a little acne. Wanted 300 pesos so I declined. I'll try her when she agrees to 200 pesos. I'm in no hurry.

Number 3 was Marisol @ Eduardo. She has great reviews and was a cutie. I said hi to Marisol and her friend Edith. I accidentally called Edith "Brenda" for some crazy reason, but Edith responded to the name Brenda. I negotiated with Marisol trying to get two positions, toda sin ropa, for 200 pesos. She said 250, I countered with 230 and thought she said okay. Turns out she meant 200 for her and 30 for hotel, she thought I said 230 for her and hotel.

We got to the room and she has her top on. I'm like, "Huh? I thought it was 230 for this."

She said, "Oh, I thought that was the hotel," and she counters with, "How about one position, toda sin ropa for 200 pesos?"

I enthusiastically agreed. From reading a lot of trip reports, I know it's super important to set a low baseline. If I am a repeat customer, eventually she'll throw in an extra position or two…

We had great conversation before, during, and after while I was fucking her, even though my Spanish sucks. She was a very sweet girl. She said she was 23, and I told her that's my lucky number and she gave a genuine laugh, not a fake laugh. Anyways, as I was fucking her for about 9 minutes and talking to her, she said *concentrado* or something so I mistakenly assumed my time was almost up. I pumped as fast as I could and came within a minute. Then I walked across the room to my cell phone and checked the time and said, "Shit! Only ten minutes! Embarrassing!!!"

She said, "No no. Es muy bueno."

I told her I usually last about 20 minutes, or 30 minutes if I'm trying. She kinda looked like she didn't like that, as I'm sure she would rather have every guy last 5 to 10 minutes and be in and out of there. That's the only warning sign I got from her. Everything else was perfect. She felt more like a friend with benefits than a hooker due to her sweetness.

I really wanted to fuck Edith @ Eduardo because of the overwhelmingly positive reviews she has but I can't get over her face even if I do her perrito. It's okay; she gets a lot more business than Marisol and I don't want Marisol to get jealous. I plan on hitting up Marisol once a week for a couple of months until I can develop her. If I can't, I'm calling it quits on that one and moving on. By develop her, I mean eventually getting her TLN, BB.

The SGs seem a lot safer due to being more like ice queens and mechanical robots, therefore most of the guys here on the board prefer bar girls because they're party girls and like the easy girls to pick up at a frat party. However, my goal as a monger is to get BBFS willingly. I've had several GFs in the past but no one was on the pill and I've never creampied a girl so that's on my bucket list. I would not creampie a girl if she's not on the pill. I may have to pay for a morning after pill or get a vasectomy first. I'm 27, not ready to have bastards.

After Marisol, I headed over to HK club to meet up with my boy. He hadn't arrived yet and I saw a stunner named Emily. She has a little gut but her pussy looked fantastic and her face is perfect. I ficha'd her two drinks and tried to negotiate. She took about 10 minutes a drink, so not fast but not slow. She wanted $80. I only had 740 pesos and she wouldn't take that. So then she had a whipped cream show with a fugly chick. Tipped lots of ones and had a great blast watching the show.

While watching the show, I decided I would get 800 pesos because she would've gone up for 800 pesos. I know it's overpaying and everyone says 600 pesos but it's a Friday night and she's a trophy fuck. We had fun while she was drinking the fichas. So after the show, I go change another $20 to pesos but she poofed. She came back an hour later but wouldn't take the 800 pesos anymore because it was very busy. She's in high demand. There goes a wasted $18 for two fichas + propina.

Anyways, so my boy finally shows up and I told him about Emily and then I caught this hot 18-year-old spinner named Kristin. Kristin is about 5' with brown hair, darker skin with lighter highlights. Super, super cute. Saw her and told friend I'd pay 600 pesos for that and he told her and she said no. Shrugged, smiled, and said no worries and was walking out then she said okay.

We go up to the hotel, pay the $15 and get to the room. Asked her if she'd do sin condom, no cum inside for 200 extra. After stalling me for 15 minutes, she realized I meant pesos and she thought it was $200 USD. Then she balks at the 600 pesos and said $60 USD to fuck. I'm like, "What the fuck? We've been in the room for fifteen minutes now," and then I was like, "Fuck it. Here's another 100 pesos," so I put 700 pesos on the table.

Oh, BTW, she asked for money first but I said after and put the money on the table.

So I finally start on her. She wouldn't kiss, didn't like DATY, didn't like me sucking on her boobs, wouldn't let me thrust fully in. It was TERRIBLE. She was worse than DFE.

She's a liar, too. Said it was her first night and then said she had many clients and then said she never kissed and all the people respect her and didn't kiss. She even said to me, "I like Filipinos and I don't like Chinos," after I asked her, "What's up? Why are you being like this? Is it because you don't like Chinos?"

Tried to snap a picture but she almost smashed my camera. Wanted to post her picture so you guys know to avoid this 18-year-old scammer super spinner. Also when I asked her how old she was, she said 18 but then asked me why and looked sketchy/annoyed. She did give me a terrible CBJ for about one minute and I stopped her and just jacked myself up to full salute because she wouldn't be able to do it with her terrible technique.

Anyways, I guess this puta saved me some money in the long run. I will never get a bar girl ever again, unless it's Monday-Wednesday for 500-600p.

So I paid 700 pesos for the worst bitch ever: Kristin—watch out. She's terrible.

At least afterwards my buddy and me went to a popular taco stand and had amazing tacos. I paid 160 pesos for dinner for both of us. We had eight tacos and two sodas. Good deal, great food. What's another 160 pesos? I thought to myself, I just got ROB'd by that puta for 700 pesos…

And then my wallet was out of pesos.

My goal: develop a SG to perform like a BG and not have to deal with all the bullshit you have to deal with in HK. In HK, you have the annoying thief meseros, the entitled bathroom attendant, the $1 robe scam, the $15 for half an hour for a hotel room, the $8 ficha + $1 tip for the ficha… all a big rip-off. I mean I paid for two fichas for Emily (super, super hot, too many guys into her) and couldn't get her to session for less than $80 USD even after the fichas even though we played around and had a good time in the booth for the 20 minutes. I will try to go on a Monday night and if she's working I'll get her; if not, no worries. I think not giving a fuck is the only way I can keep from becoming a PLM.

My goal to achieve my plan: workout hard for the next two months to get my six-pack back. Treat the SGs with kindness and respect and follow the advice on giving them little gifts and such for their kids. I want to be like the Amigo who knows how to blur the line between client/novio, but I'll never become a novio because I know where that leads. I want to do this with SGs not BGs because they are cleaner, harder to develop, and much more bang for your buck!

Don't You Remember Me?

CRIP

Most of us have probably had a chica approach that you either never noticed or had the slightest interest in and use the come-on line that you were once arriba'd with her and it was hot off the charts. While you scratch your head wondering if you might know her or if you ever could have been drunk enough to fuck this chica, you get the incredulous "You don't remember me?" So the chica vendor gets her foot in the door and is able to make a pitch to get your interest no matter how much you are sure that you never talked to her before. It's a harmless sales trick used almost exclusively by more desperate old and/or doggie looking chicas who need to rely on resourcefulness since their looks won't get your attention.

Last week, I experienced a funny new wrinkle on this harmless old scam. I know a chica who had been working a non-sex job while living undocumented in LA. After losing the gig, she voluntarily ran back to Mexico because her kids were in Mexico. Finding herself a fichera in Tropical, she realizes instantly that she should have stayed in the US, and from Day 1 is looking for a PLM to get engaged to and to get her back north legally.

She is 30 or close to it, but cute enough, and noticed me checking her out as she ficha'd with another guy. When he left, she came over and asked for a drink. After three minutes at my table, she was already presenting an insane novia proposal and I knew this was one loca chica. I shut her down.

From then on, when I came to BT, she knew I was no longer a candidate for her game and sharked me only for business and we had some fun on that basis. After driving away many other BT gringo clients with her fast track novia-ing, she figures out that if she's going to be trapped in Mexico, she may as well just become a full-fledged and well-paid high volume puta, and so has made the logical move to AB.

Which brings us to last Wednesday. I am sitting at a table in AB when a very cute young chica who I can't recall seeing anywhere at anytime—and this is one I would remember—comes over to my table and swallows me with a big hug and kiss and greets me using my first name. I'm wondering who the fuck is this and hesitating and I get: "Don't you remember me? I'm Debbie and we had good times at Tropical together in the past!" I'm scratching my last few hairs out of my head as she repeatedly uses my name.

I mean, this chica is NICE and I could not forget her if I had been with her. I once had a wild afternoon described in an old TR with a BT chica who is often referred to as "Dirty Debbie", but Her Dirtiness did not earn her handle by being seriously young and cute. I know Dirty Debbie well and this fresh young muffin is no Dirty Debbie. Then there is Deborah who was a BT mainstay for a long time before moving to AB a few years ago, so I know it ain't Deborah who is just a few paces away at that particular time. But Debbie's use of my name has me stumped—it would seem she really does know me!

So anyhow Debbie is cute enough and it doesn't matter really whether I have known her before or not, but also this is not the time to get with her since I have other locked-in plans and I'm just killing time at AB. So after a decent number of apologies for not remembering her and telling her she's cute and maybe I can give her a chance to refresh my memory at a later date, she relents and walks away. I watch her walk to the deepest, darkest recesses of the bar from where I'm perched. I see her plant purposefully next to another chica, obviously an amiga, and they start yabbering immediately. But dark or not, I now see that the amiga she's blah blah'ing with is none other then the notorious Tropical novia-ter who knows that my time with her is done!!!

So a nice smart new wrinkle on the old harmless, "You don't remember me?" scam—get the monger's name from an amiga to gain credibility, and probably the amiga gets a finder's fee if the monger bites on the bait.

Hopefully my next report about Debbie will be a chica report and not a scam report.

Amigo Commentary

DATSALLWRONG: Why didn't you tell her that you remember her? Tell her you remember she gave your free sessions and bareback all the time and make it a point that she always liked to swallow, too.

FREAKPROPHET: Tell her you remember her well and ask her for the $20 you loaned her.

SFSCULPTO: What makes you think the friend was working a non-sex job in LA? Just because she said she was a bartender doesn't mean shit. She didn't end up a whore by accident. In LA, I think she was working as a whore in a Mexican dive and she found out she could make more in TJ and deal with a better class of people so she came here.

CRIP: You guys think just like me since those are the exact kind of responses I use in most of these situations. This time was different since her use of my name and her appearance being right in my kitchen as to the kind of chicas I like made me think that she might be on the level.

And I don't know or care what she was doing in LA. I'm just reporting what she told me. I did tend to believe her since she didn't seem whoreiented—choosing to park at BT instead of AB and working the novia angle over the let's-go-to-the-room angle. She also insists that she's from Columbia, but the father of her kid or kids is Mexican. Again, I don't know what is real and what is fiction and I don't give a damn or feel any need to press an investigation.

JimmyTJ: Is this Camilia formerly of BT? I do not hang out in AB but I heard she was working over there. She told me she used to bartend in LA.

I sat with her once in BT. I was standing right inside BT surveying my options; she had a waiter ask me to buy her a drink. I should have said no, but pickings were not great that night. We grabbed a table in the back. A few minutes later, a crazy gringo came charging at our table. He had his hand outstretched with a fistful of money. Camilia met him about ten feet from our table. He had the look of love and PLM'ness in his eyes. It looked like I had taken his love away.

I thought maybe I would have to fight this PLM fucker. Camilia had him escorted out of BT. She came back to me and I said, "You have a crazy novio." I should have just dumped her at that point, but we hung out a little while in BT then went to Cantina de Panochas where she sings karaoke. I gave her my number and she called and texted numerous times but I never responded to her. I avoided BT for a few weeks because I did not want to deal with her. When I finally came back, she acted like she owned me, talking smack to other chicas that I sat with. Crazy chica. Never did fuck her.

ALL IN THE FAMILY

BYRON

So I did something wild with Bella. A little background on this chica. She is 19, 5' 4", 100lbs, pale skin, and possibly the prettiest chica I ever met in TJ. She sort of looks like a young Uma Thurman. She would pass as a gringa with flying colors. She lived and went to school in San Diego when she was at age 9-11, so she speaks English with natural accent, although her vocabulary is limited.

When we first met, she decided she would be my girlfriend. I took her to Rosarito and Ensenada. She has a 21-year-old sister working in the same bar. They are from Sinaloa where their 37-year-old mother also works at bar. Officially, her mom is a mesera, but Bella tells me she goes up.

The mother decided to come to TJ to visit her daughters. She was going to be here for a week, but wouldn't just sit around in a hotel room. She might as well make ficha money by working at the bar. Bella told me she knew about me and wanted to meet me.

The first night the mother arrived, she introduces me as her novio. I sit with her and two daughters. I try to behave like a nice respectable BF. The mother doesn't speak a word of English. I don't stay long with the three.

The second night, I sit with Bella. She tells me her mother thinks I am very guapo. *That's a good thing to hear,* I say to myself, *though I am here to fuck you, Bella.* I ask her if she wants to go up.

She says she can't, because she is having her period.

Damn. I didn't expect this. So I jokingly ask her, "Can I go with another chica then?"

Bella is not amused.

After a moment of hesitation, I say, "How about if I go with your mother?"

To my surprise, Bella gets excited. She tells me that's a great idea. She would rather see me going with her than any other chica, her sister included. The mother will not compete with her because, among other reasons, she will be here only for a week. "My mom will go with you today. Next week, I will go with you." These are her exact words. Besides, the mother needs money and can make some this way, she says.

Now you guys reading this might think this is crazy. If I were you, I would think the same. Being there, though, I could make some sort of rationalization… well, to a degree. The way how I saw it, I was giving the mother a huge compliment by taking her up. I was saying, basically, she was attractive enough for me to pay. That's what the women who work in the bar value, I surmise.

From my point, I don't deny I had a kinky thought of doing mother-daughter combo thing. But that was not all. I actually wanted to befriend myself with the mother so that I would have a better chance with Bella. The family support is always a nice thing. Like they say, "If you want to gain a girl's heart, try to gain her mother's," or something like that.

I ask Bella if she wants to talk with the mother about this idea.

She jumps up from her chair, walks to her mother, talks with her, and comes back with her. Bella mediates our "negotiation" as an interpreter. Bella asks me how long I'd like to stay with her. I say 30 minutes. I then ask her how much the mother wants. They speak to each other. 70 bucks.

That's a hefty fee for a 37-year-old woman, but I am talking about a family obligation here. I say, "Fine. Let's go."

I take the mother's hand and we walk toward the bar exit together. Bella and her sister giggle as we walk out. I feel eyes of many other chicas upon us. We go upstairs to the hotel reception. The guy who attends the desk knows I go with Bella. He looks amused to see the mother and I checking in.

We enter a room. I start telling her how much I like her daughter. She understands my elementary Spanish. This is getting awkward, but there is no return. We get naked. The mother is skinny with small breasts. Her face strongly resembles her daughter's though. The same beautiful eyes. Looks 6.5. I have got to be generous with this one. Fuckable, nonetheless.

She starts with BBBJ. Very nice one. The skill of a mother of six children (all daughters) cannot be underestimated. I might rate the technique 8 just for her BBBJ. It is now time for sexo. I usually ask a chica to start on top. The mother, however, orders me to be on top. I have no choice.

This is the point when something I vaguely knew becomes obvious. I MUST impress her with my sexual prowess. My reputation in the family is at stake. So, I pull every trick in my book to entertain the mother. She likes it. She moans and screams, and gives DFK in between. She puts her nails on my back as I hump her. She cums. Twice. I would usually call this type of session GFE. This one is a GFME.

After sexo, she tells me how lucky her daughter is because I am such a good lover. She repeats this, like, ten times. She then says I should visit Sinaloa. Or, even better, move there so that I will live with her, Bella, and five other daughters. I laugh. That will be too much. I tell her I will take care of her daughter here, though.

So evidently, I manage to gain the mother's heart. In the ZN style, I guess.

I Thought It Was Love Until...

VARIOUS

Ivanho: My guess is there are at least a few guys on this board who can complete this sentence: *I thought it was love until...*

So I was down there for a couple days this week. I meet a new BG and met up with her both nights as soon as her shift ended. We went out drinking and dancing 'til the wee hours and had wild sex filled with passion as the sun came up.

I THOUGHT IT WAS LOVE UNTIL she showed me a text message she had tried to send me and I noticed my contact name in her phone was USA GRINGO #7.

Haus: I know how you feel Amigo, from Pendejo #5.

Nayarit: I'm listed in my amiga's phone as Don... as in Don Julio or Don Francisco.

Cuernitos: Don means "old fart" in Mexico. "Ahi viene el don" means "Here comes the old fart." It can also be used as the equivalent of "Mr." Now if you don't happen to be old, your chica respects you a lot.

HereandThere: Could be worse. Try Judio Moreno.

Ranchero1: I guess it could have been worse when you looked in her contacts and found yourself listed as "Pendejo #19".

But I like the Zona chicas who are greedy and self-serving because it makes them predictable so that you can play them for as long as it amuses you before you give her the boot in the ass telling her that her pussy is rotten and she gives lousy head.

Ahh yes, there is nothing more satisfying than to watch a whore in the zone go ballistic over her realizing that you have been playing her for a fool all along before she got a chance to cash in on your being too gullible to figure out what she was planning all along.

It's all part of the game in the zone with these girls in that you gotta think several steps ahead of her to stay up.

CHITOWNLAWYER: Frankly, having been involved in a lot of civie relationships over the past 40 years, I can see how there could be something refreshingly transparent about a P4P relationship. With paid company, the terms of trade on both side of the transaction are clear, and there is much less room for misunderstanding.

No hearing, "If you loved me, you'd know." Or, just to take an example, trying to sort out a situation in which she pretends to have a friendship with another woman, but she really dislikes her. Do I need to pretend to like that woman as well, so that there is a united front? Or do I need to show my loyalty to "my" woman by disliking the other woman? Can I say that I dislike that other woman, or would that be interpreted as disrespectful to "my" woman, who pretends to like the other woman (although "my" woman really dislikes the other woman)…?

This is only one example of the complete bullshit that arises from emotional relationships with women. P4P is much more straightforward and direct: I give you $X for Y period of time, during which time you French kiss me/let me suck your boobs/let me eat you out/suck my dick, let me fuck you/take it up the ass for me while saying "meow" like Hello Kitty, etc. End of story.

Unfortunately, there seems to be some need for emotional connection, which is why we have threads like this.

HEREANDTHERE: We have that need in the Zona? I thought we just had delusions and illusion!

BIC54: Does anybody know what "Pene Enorme" means? Four of my favoritas in HK have saved my number under that name.

JonSilencio: Two possible meanings here:

1) You have one

~or~

2) You are one!

Only she and her real BF know for sure!

Bic54: There's no question which one I am.

JonSilencio: Bic54, mi amigo, just having a little fun! A monger buddy of mine met a BG who had regular customer names stored in her phone with the $ amounts they paid her, ranked in descending order from highe$t to lowe$t.

If I show up on a chica's list as 'Gringo A$$hole #1', is that a good thing or a bad thing?

Bic54: JS, I appreciate the humor. Everything I do on this site is for fun. As soon as it's not, I'll have to reconsider a few things.

As for Gringo Asshole… as long as I'm #1, I could live with that.

HereandThere: I thought it was love 'til I realized I had no idea what her actual name was, how old she was, and I had no interest whatsoever in finding out.

Ivanho: So it's been a few weeks since we first met. I was back in the Zona yesterday. My plan was to avoid the bar she works in and just drink with the fellas. But you know how things change when you drink. So I send a drunk text and the next thing I know she shows up. I didn't even remember if I told her where I was, but I guess I did.

So we drink for a couple hours and then head to the purple hotel for sex. But the strange part comes when she drags me in to Play Boy to meet her sister. After we meet, we are sitting there and she looks around to make sure no one is listening and then she whispers, "My sister is a prostituta." Jajajaja! What should I say? "I know she is, but what are you?"

X-Wiz: Something like that had happened to me few years ago… I was showing a BG our message conversation and she saw that I named her Elizabeth#5. Needless to say she was pissed off but she quickly calmed down when I said, "No, that is your 5th number because you always lose or have your smartphone stolen!"

LatinMILFLover: X-Wiz, nice recovery. If I could be THAT quick, it may have saved me from one divorce.

I was out drinking one night after work in 1978 and happened to catch the eye of a very nice Asian woman in the bar. I took her to my car and we had sex in the parking lot of the bar.

When I got home, my wife was sleeping. I thought I should clean myself up and get the odor of pussy off of me in the event my wife wanted to have sex in the morning. As I am washing the smell off of my penis, my wife enters the bathroom and asks what I am doing. I wanted to say *I did not want to wake you up and was masturbating*, but what came out was, "Eh… ah… umm… nothing, honey." A long and costly divorce followed. But I did have the Asian GF for almost a year before she moved back to Seattle.

Belgrath: I thought I was in love until… the one time I miscalculated and didn't have enough pesos left for a taxi to the border and she wouldn't give me 50 pesos back out of the 1250 pesos I gave her. I had to walk back to the border at 3am.

SS: Now that's a reality check.

JoseTejas: I found out my name on my girl's phone. It was Jose Ch. "Ch" for "Cheater" because she knows I am married.

Joe Average: Thought it was love until she got pregnant by another monger… he just saved me a shit load of money!

Belgrath: Just like the insurance commercial… "I just saved a bunch of money by switching to Gloria…"

A Week in Tijuana

mic

Two things I learned from my trip: I prefer the massage parlors over the bar scene. Threesomes and foursomes are nice, but overrated. One-on-one is best.

I flew into San Diego last Friday. I had some business there that week. I've been reading the posts here for the better part of a year, and all you guys have inspired me to go on a little adventure.

The one major obstacle I had was time, not money. I flew down with a whole team of people from my company, and I knew it'd be a challenge to get away from them for enough quality time in Tijuana.

So on Saturday, it took me a few hours, but I was able to ditch everyone, and headed down to the border at about 11pm. I parked at one of the lots and walked over. For some reason, I started off being cheap. I spotted the arch at the end of Revolución and decided to walk, instead of catching a cab. Stupid. Not only did it take me nearly 30 minutes to get there, but I was tired, and there were too many dark alleys. My advice? Just pay the $5 cab fare.

Anyway, I found Zona Norte easily and went in and out most of the bars. Both CC and AB were packed. I didn't see many free girls in CC, so I walked down to AB. It was so crowded, I had to wait behind about a dozen dudes to get in. There were plenty of girls, but no place to sit, and I was in no mood to run in a rat race.

This was my first time down there, and I admit to being a little overwhelmed.

I don't remember much about most of the other bars, except that I wasn't very much impressed with either the places or the girls. Well, I do remember two of the bars: HK and Rio Rosa's. HK had some two-girl show going on. Nice, but I couldn't see because it was so crowded with dudes. Every other girl I saw was with some guy. So I rolled. Rosa's was practically empty. I found a table in a dark corner, and ordered a Coke. I was sleepy, horny, and very disappointed. I had money to spend, but I sure as hell wasn't in the mood to put forth a whole bunch of effort to get laid. And then these fat ugly women from Rosa's kept coming up to me while I was trying to relax. It was too much so I left and found a cab.

I was ready to go back to the border. The driver asked me if I wanted to get a massage, of course. I thought a moment, and then told him yes. I found out later that he took me to Mermaids. It is a nice place. You go upstairs to the second floor where there's a bar and plenty of leather couches to lounge on. There were a couple of girls hanging out, but mostly what looked like locals having a drink. Some guy took me to a side room, where five women promptly walked in and introduced themselves. I picked Jasmine and Erica for full service for one hour.

Erica was beautiful by any standard. About 5'3" and slim. She was well-proportioned, nice sized breasts, flat stomach, and a round ass. Her hair was dyed some golden color with highlights, which was a little short of shoulder length. Her facial features were more European than the other girls, small narrow nose, straight thin lips, and here eyes were some kind of light brownish color. Hey, don't give me a hard time. My wife says I am colorblind after all. Jasmine was bigger in the bust and the hips, but still proportional, which is very important to me.

They took me downstairs, outside, and into a building next door, where I paid $60 for a nice room. It was a large room, with a Jacuzzi along the back wall, a bathroom with a shower in the corner, and a full-sized bed along one of the side walls. Erica told me they wanted $80 each, so I paid them. I could see in her eyes she regretted offering just $80. She tried to say $100 real quick, and I told her no. But just before they put their money away, I gave them each an extra $20. Hell, I had the money. I didn't need them upset with me before we started.

Anyway, we got disrobed, jumped in the tub, and got to rubbing each other all over with bubbles. Man, this was a fantasy come true! Sitting in a hot tub, Jasmine sucking my dick, and me sucking Erica's well formed tits with my finger in her pussy. Nice.

Neither could speak much English, and my high school Spanish is all but forgotten. But I was able to tell them it was time to start fucking. Erica got out, but for some reason, Jasmine pushed me back in the tub and straddled me right there. She rode me for about ten minutes before she came. I didn't though. Nothing makes me feel more satisfied than watching a woman I'm fucking have an orgasm. It sure strokes the ego. Anyway, Jasmine walked into the shower with a twinkle in her eye, and a satisfied smile on her face. *Yeah, who's your daddy!*

Erica wasn't as good of a fuck. First of all, she complained that I was too big. I thought at first that she was trying to compliment me, but realized she really was complaining. I laid her on her back and went to town. She stopped me and turned around and got on her knees. That was nice, but then she stopped again, pushed me on my back, and got atop me. She said something about having only five more minutes. Well, I'd had enough. I asked for Jasmine again.

I propped her up on her knees, and took her from behind. I don't understand what Erica's problem was, Jasmine was smaller, but was definitely enjoying sex much more than Erica was. I thought no more of Erica and concentrated on Jasmine. She didn't rush me. I took my time, and I made her climax again, and this time so did I. Nice, real nice. The cabby took me back to the border, and I drove back to my hotel in San Diego.

I couldn't get away from my colleagues until about 7pm Sunday evening. I parked my car at the lot, and this time I took a taxi to Zona Norte. I walked into AB and it was still happening. Plenty of girls and plenty of guys, but there was some seating. I was there only for about ten minutes when one Griselda approached me. Long shapely legs captured my eyes, and I followed them up to a very short, tight mini skirt. Big round breasts and pretty face with blonde hair to top it off. She looked good, so I bought her a drink. Now this is what I wanted (or so I thought), a beautiful woman walking up to me, asking what it is I wanted to do to her. Fucky and Sucky for $60. Sure, I can dig it. She took me next door and up the stairs. I paid the prick behind the desk $11, and remembered to ask for an extra towel.

We found a room, and Griselda wasted no time. She started peeling off her clothes, and then I realized this was no young chica. Oh, she was beautiful, but she just had some wrinkles here and there. No problem. She pushed me on the bed. I sucked her tits, fingered her pussy, and then she sat on me. However, it soon became apparent to me she was a veteran. Sure, she moaned and groaned, said "Fuck me, papi," and all that, but she never smiled, and her eyes never lit up. And her pussy was very loose. I almost didn't feel like I was having sex. She said something about the time, so I flipped her over on her back, and tried my best to nail her through the bed. Still, no response.

But I came. Still, I felt like the whore. Used and abused, and only good for one thing. She walked over to the sink, splashed some water between her legs, and she was putting her clothes back on. I told myself then that I would never again go with a bar girl who approached me. I wanted no more part of veterans. Damn!

Well, I couldn't get back to Tijuana until Wednesday. I not only had business obligations, but social ones as well. Two nights in a row I had to go bar-hopping in San Diego in the Gaslamp district with my client and some coworkers. Really put a cramp in my efforts at mongering in TJ.

But late Wednesday afternoon, I rolled out of dodge with the quickness, straight down to the border. First place I go is AB. Place is still jumpin'. And plenty of girls to choose from. I order a Coke, and start checking out every girl in the bar. A few come up to me, but I politely decline their services. No more veterans for me!

I'm thinking today that I want another threesome, AB style. Just when I narrowed my choices down to two girls, one of them walks out with two of her friends, and when I turn to look for my other choice, she's gone as well. I'm pissed, and hitting myself in the side of the head. There are still plenty of hot girls still there, but I had my eyes set on those two. Damn! So I get up and leave.

I walked around the block, went through the alley, checked out a few bars, but none of them had as many nice looking girls as AB. I walked back into AB to see if my dream girls had come back. I did see one come back, sit down, and a couple minutes later go back out with some dude. Okay, I know these girls have a lot of mileage, but I'm not sure I wanted one who just got finished fucking two guys in less than a hour. So I was down to one.

I wait a while longer, feeling more frustrated, and I walk out again to go over to CC. Before I get there, I'm accosted by this dude on the corner trying to convince me that bars are a waste of my time, and that I should go to a massage parlor. The girls are cleaner, and the experience is less rushed.

Well, in my limited experience, I agreed with him, but today I wanted a bar threesome. However, he's persistent so I allow him to take me to La Tropa and then Deja Vu. There were some pretty girls in there, but I'm now fixated on the one I lost. So I finally wander into CC, and it's dead. There's about three girls in there. That's it. Now I'm just pissed. I go to the bar to order a drink, and one of the girls walks over, grabs my dick, and asks if I want a suck.

No dear, I'm a little keyed up right now. I have to relax. She tries a little while longer, then walks off.

I take a deep breath and walk back over to AB. There she is. Beautiful girl, about 5', wearing tight blue jeans and a black bra (halter top? whatever). She's got short black hair with blue highlights, and oh, what a dazzling smile. I waste no time. I tap her on the shoulder and ask her is she wants to sit down with me. Did I say that she's got a beautiful smile? We talk a bit, her name is Patricia; she's from some small town near Mexico City. I tell her I want her for an hour, she tells me it's $22 for the room, and $100 for her. Then I tell her my fantasy of a threesome. No problem! $50 for each of them. I let her call her friend over, Lorena. I wouldn't have picked her, somewhat wide in the waist, but still a pair of breasts and a pussy on legs. We get upstairs, and it dawns on me that I agreed to just 30 minutes, not an hour. Damn, well I guess I'd better make quick work of them then.

Lorena took her clothes off, and I see stuff just sagging. Oh man! The miracles tight clothes will perform. Sagging breasts, sagging stomach, cottage cheese legs. At least Patricia is still hot. She pulls her pants off, and there's a big thick, long scar from one hip to the other. I'm not feeling any mojo. Then I look at her beautiful face, with that smile, check out her firm breasts and stomach. Ignore scar, admire her ass and legs. Okay! I'm back in the game.

Needless to say, it was Patricia whom I did first. I put her on her back, and while slowing plunging in and out, I did take advantage of another pussy nearby to stick my finger in. Yeah, I was taking my time, feeling up Lorena, sucking her tits, then Patricia's, then Lorena's again. I was having fun. Then Patricia makes me stop, and there's a small puddle of blood on the bed. I quickly check, condom still intact. When she gets up, Lorena quickly folds the sheet over, and pulls another one down, switches condoms and lays on her back inviting me in.

I'm thinking, "Poor Patricia!" She was smiling the whole time, but I could tell she was a little uncomfortable. I'm still hard, but not into it anymore. Lorena starts trying to make me cum. She flips me over on my back and starts calling me papi, moaning, grabbing my balls.

Will someone tell these ladies that grabbing a man's balls while she's jumping up and down on his dick at 60rpm is not the best way to make him shoot his wad? Erica was doing the same thing.

Needless to say, I didn't cum. When Patricia comes back out of the bathroom, Lorena says the time's up.

I'm really disappointed. So I ask if they could just suck my dick. Poor pretty Patricia tries, but she's not into it. I put my hand on the back of her head to help her along, and then notice that fine black hair with the blue highlights is a wig. She's done, her smile is gone, and she is now not so attractive to me. I wonder how long ago she had the c-section, which is what I assume the problem was. In the end, I gave them both a $10 tip. They tried at least. I feel dirty for a different reason. No more AB for me.

Now I didn't drive all the way down to Tijuana from San Diego not to cum. I get in a cab and ask the driver to take me to Maria Bonita's massage. The guy on the corner claimed that was the best massage parlor. The driver acted like he didn't understand what I meant and kept saying that Monte Carlo was the best. At this point, I didn't really much care. I just wanted a decent massage and to stick my dick inside a beautiful girl. I found out later that week that Maria Bonita's was shut down that same day.

Anyway, Monte Carlo had a few really pretty girls. I chose Cynthia. She had dark shoulder length hair, and a pretty innocent looking face, small breasts, but a fat ass! She wore tight white pants, with cutouts all up and down her legs. And she wore a white lace blouse, that was practically see-through. Oh yes!

I paid $42 for the room for one hour. Cynthia took me to a very small room, big enough only for a small table, an armchair and the massage table. I wanted sex, but I also wanted to relax, so I let her give me a massage, and we didn't discuss anything else. Well, the massage was good, well worth the $42. After some time, she said she was finished, and wanted to know if I wanted any other service.

I was feeling good, so I thought I'd try to make a joke. There was a red sign on the wall stating (in Spanish) in essence that asking for and giving sex was prohibited by law. So I pointed it out to her, and she just smiled, and said to pay no attention to it. If I wanted full service, it was $130. Fellas, I chickened out. I had the money, but $130 was steep. I was silent for about a minute, and Cynthia calmly asked, "Sí o no?" I caved. I gave her the $130.

She dutifully peeled off her clothes while I watched in anticipation. She didn't complain about my size. In fact, she didn't even speak. As I lay on the table, she mounted me, facing away. She must have known I liked her big ass. I locked on to those cheeks, one in each hand, and started rocking her. Now, this was my sixth chica in five days, and I think I had gotten an education in judging whether the girl was enjoying herself or just faking it. Well, Cynthia wasn't just ramming my cock into her pussy, she was having sex, and enjoying it. Which made the experience for me worth it. I asked her to turn around. I wanted to see her face. Oh, she was definitely into it. She closed her eyes, bit her trembling lower lip. *Yes, yes, I could take her.*

I flipped her over on her back, and started pumping, slowly. In the end, I was a very satisfied man, not just because I came into her, but because I felt she was really enjoying herself. I would have given her a tip, had I not already blown $130 on her, and the fact that I had no idea where I was, and needed to pay a taxi driver to get me back to the border. We both wrapped a towel around ourselves, and we walked to a large bathroom with a large shower. We got in together. I was so satisfied I didn't even think about feeling her up some more. I left Tijuana that evening around 7pm with mixed feelings. I definitely overpaid, but I guess I got exactly what I paid for.

Thursday, I couldn't get away. I found myself in a bar in Pacific Beach with a coworker, and a bunch of his friends. I have no idea which bar. We just walked up and down Grand Ave checking out one place after another. After a while, the group broke up, and I found myself talking to some drunk girl name Melissa. She was attractive enough, but she was the leftover half of a pair, the hotter one hanging all over my buddy Reid. Short, a little more than five feet, with long dark, curly hair, Melissa's face was a little chubby, but that drunken smile and dark glassy eyed wondrous stare was adorable. I really was just humoring the girl in the hopes that Reid would get laid before his flight, which was just a few hours away. Melissa's more attractive friend was Kara. She was stunning, long straight blonde hair, classic model's face, and a body to go with it. I would give Melissa a 7, maybe, but Kara was a definite 9.

Kara was so into Reid, that when the bar closed (they all close at the ridiculously early time of 1:30), she invited us back to her condo. *Surprise, surprise, I was going to have sex for free!* I didn't even have to buy any drinks.

It seemed to take forever navigating those dark streets. The girls were acting goofy and were very talkative. I don't talk much, but I had incentive that night to keep both girls in good spirits, at least until I got what I wanted. Melissa went on and on about her boyfriend who was serving on the USS Reagan. *Sorry Gary, maybe you should get a job that doesn't take you away for so many weeks at a time.*

Anyway, Kara's place was really small. One bedroom, which left the living room for me and Melissa. That was just fine. Melissa kept on talking, while I took pains to get her pants off. She and Kara are from North Carolina, and she claims she's always wanted to have sex with a black man. Well, then, let's get to it.

By now, I gathered I was a little bigger than the average dude. I've had four of six chicas react in varying degrees of annoyance and delight. After getting a towel for the couch, I laid her back and began removing her blouse. It was some kind of v-neck vest looking thing made out of satin.

Well, I was surprised, this little girl had a tight body! Initially, I couldn't really tell with the loose blouse and her baggy jeans. But I'd found a diamond in the rough here! After I'd gotten her completely nude, I stood back for a moment to admire her body. A definite 8!

She called me "boy" and told me to hurry up. Who was I to complain? I wasn't about to be sensitive now, so I stripped naked. I started licking her nipples and went down to her pussy. What I dared not do in Tijuana, I felt no qualms about doing now. I had just started getting going, she was nice and wet and sloppy now, when she said "Nigger, fuck me!" I knew she meant it as a term of endearment, and if not, who cares?

As usual, I started slow. I don't know how long we went at it in that same position, but nothing makes this brother feel more on top of his game than to fuck a woman into sweaty hysterics and gasping for breath. She locked her arms around my neck and her legs around my back and wouldn't let go for a long time. I tried to pull out a few times, but each time, she let out a spasm and wouldn't let go. So I just lay there on top of her. At some point I must've fallen asleep, because near dawn, Reid woke me up. He was already dressed. I got my stuff on, and we said goodbye to the girls. I was curious, so I asked Melissa if she remembered calling me any names. In answer, she grabbed the back of my neck and stuck her tongue in my mouth so fast, I almost choked. Then she bit my lip and whispered in my ear, "Boy, you did good."

I wonder if I spoiled her for Gary. You all know that saying, "Once you go black..." Anyway, all we had to do now was figure out where hell we were so that I could find my car and get Reid to the airport in time. Very memorable.

So now it was Friday, and my flight out of town was Saturday morning. One more night in Tijuana. I almost didn't make it. I had a long last day and was looking forward to fraternizing with a few more chicas. But I forgot that I had promised another friend of mine that I would meet him in downtown San Diego. Some kind of way, I found myself back up in Pacific Beach. Had a good time, and almost forgot about Tijuana. Manuel, being a good friend, wanted me to crash on his sofa. He'd make sure I made my flight.

I could not do this. I'm not sure how, but I convinced Manuel to let me drive to my hotel. I would talk to him on my cell phone all the way back to the hotel, about a fifteen-minute drive. He went for it, and I did actually drive back to my hotel, but after I hung up the phone, I was on the road again. It was after 3am, not much time. I suppose I was stupid to drive, as tired and full of liquor as I was. But I was on a mission, dammit!

Somewhere along the way to the border, I got in my mind the idea of trying a foursome, tres chicas. And I wanted two hours, not one. Well, it was late in the night, and a lot of the girls were going home. I went over to Deja Vu. They had plenty of girls, but only one, maybe two that I was feeling a vibe from. Then I went back to Mermaids. They had one looker and a bunch of fat girls. Oh, where was Jasmine? So I ended up in Luxor. I knew they were expensive, but this is where the girls were. The lineup had a dozen girls at 4am. They were closing at 5am, so they wouldn't let me pay for two hours. Sense almost took over. I picked this girl name Paulina. Sweet looking girl, cute innocent seeming smile. Wearing a short white skirt and a matching white tube top. Something kept nagging me about her. Like I recognized here from somewhere. Anyway, my desperation for a new adventure overrode common sense, and I told them I wanted three girls. There was a bit of commotion, and I could hear the girls' surprise from behind the little glass wall they have. They marched the girls back out, and I picked a hard bodied Melissa (coincidence) and a petite Julie. Julie looked almost American, which is probably why I chose her instead of another hard-bodied Latina. Hey, variety is the spice of life!

I paid $120 for the room, $40 for each girl. Paulina led me outside, and around to some side door. I was still wondering what it was about Paulina that seemed so familiar. We finally went into a large room, with a large Jacuzzi and a table. No beds like Mermaids. Paulina disappeared and Melissa and Julie came in. I stated my intentions of fucking all three girls. Melissa, whose English was very good, didn't believe me. "All three? Are you sure?" Yes, yes! $120 each. Yes, I am a fool, but money is meant to be spent. Okay, deal. Paulina comes back. Girls, take your clothes off. Melissa starts sucking my dick, and I take turns licking Julie's tiny breasts and Paulina's small but perky ones. While at the same time fingering both of them. That's when Melissa and Julie start with the "You're too big!"

Yeah, Julie, you first. Poor girl, I WAS too big for her. I could feel it; she was just too tight for me to fit. She only lowered herself about halfway down before she was grimacing in pain. So I ignored her and kept fondling the other two beautiful girls willing to let me put my fingers up their pussies and suck on their nipples. Abruptly, Julie got up. I guess she had had enough. Well, so did I. Next!

Melissa mounted me. I was surprised how much she complained about how big I was. Telling a brother he's got a huge dick is a stroke to one's ego, but a constant reminder that he's too big is a turn off. She got me all the way in there, but she was moving way too fast. So I put her on her knees and hit her from behind.

But I kept looking at Paulina. That thing about her kept bugging me. My eyes kept going back to her face. Each time, she'd give me a shy little smile, no doubt wondering what the hell I was thinking. Julie was useless at this point. She was watching porn on the TV, not at all paying attention to me. At least Paulina was there rubbing my ass. I knew it was time to switch when Melissa started with the fake "Fuck me, papi" bit.

Dammit, I think must have hurt Melissa, too. How is it these prostitutes can have tight pussies?

So I pulled out and quietly called Paulina to me.

Well, I just laid Paulina on her back and took her missionary style on top of the table. Slow, steady strokes as I stared into her eyes. She looked back into my eyes, she didn't say a thing, and she smiled that shy smile of hers. This one's a keeper. After a few minutes, she was really into it, rocking with me, hands on my hips.

Then it dawns on me! She is a Latina carbon copy of Jennifer Aniston. Okay, a little wider in the face, but the resemblance is unmistakable. I quicken the pace a bit. This girl knows how to enjoy sex. I pull her legs up over my shoulders and try to get as deep as I can. The deed is done.

Paulina gets up, and I lay on the table in her place in exhaustion. My hour isn't up, so I ask them to give me a massage. I close my eyes and revel in the sensation of six hands running all over my naked body. After a few minutes, I noticed the hands on my left side all but disappear. Julie, again, watching TV. So I grab her ass, and start fingering her again. Paulina is on my right. She gives me that shy smile again. Oh yes, Paulina is definitely a keeper. And Melissa is at my head, giving me a perfect perspective from which to inspect her perfect breasts. I reach around to grab her ass, run my hand up her back and force her forward so that I could lick her nipples again. I close my eyes again and sigh. It's time to go, before I get too sleepy. Before I sit up, I give Paulina one more squeeze of the ass and caress of the breast. I give them each a hug and say thank you. Yes, even Julie.

Melissa asks if I would like to buy them a gift, or give a tip. I almost laugh. My excuse is that I need enough money to get back to the border. And Paulina asks why I can't walk. So is she upset that I wanted to fuck three girls instead of just her? I found out shortly thereafter that she was right. I could have just walked. I paid $5 for a taxi to drive me 100 yards.

I catch my flight and take a taxi home from the airport. Of course, I've been away from my wife for eight days. I get home and the woman attacks me. Two hours later, we're both sweaty and exhausted. After all that, sex is best at home.

Executive Summary:
$260 to fuck Jasmine & Erica in a Jacuzzi and a proper bed: A
$71 to fuck Griselda and feel like the dirty whore: C
$142 to fuck poor Patricia and loosy Lorena: D
$172 to fuck Cynthia and get a real massage: A
$0 to ravage young Melissa in PB: A
$480 to live a foursome fantasy w/ Paulina, Melissa & Julie: B+

Amigo Commentary

DrChoi: Wow, you went all out. Now, what was the problem with the big dick?

Ben: Something you'll never have to worry with, Choi!

DrChoi: I have problems with loose pussy.

GringoRich: There is one girl famous for being very expensive at Mermaids. She is hot and will not go up for less than $120 package. That means $80 for her. That does not mean $120 for her in the room. Package always means room and service included and nothing is negotiated with the girl. Everyone else works on a package for $100. Even the meseros know her as the chica that will not go up for less than $120 ($80 to her and $40 to the house for the room). She is also famous for having the worst service even though she charges the most.

That explains to me that any negotiated session inside the room with the girl is just to see how much extra you are willing to pay. This is not advised for the newcomer to MPs. You can pay extra. But if you were to pay more than necessary, at least try to negotiate some extras beforehand to justify it. But tipping in MPs is like tipping in AB or CC. It is not common. I don't tip as a rule, but there are exceptions. If the girl does the minimum or less, forget it.

BTW, showers together, actual massages, and spending a full hour is considered normal. This is the appeal of MPs.

So the moral of the story is $80 (to girl) is considered very expensive. $60 (to girl) is the norm. This is regarding the package deal. If you don't get the package, then the girls will hit you up for $120 for them only ($160 including the price of the room). They ask just to see if you will pay it. Don't.

Á la carte, rooms are $40 for a standard. $60 for a Jacuzzi suite. This is only if you don't get the package. Always get the package. I am shuddering about hearing charges of $120 for a room only. But it appeared as if our monger paid $240 for an all-inclusive package for three. Not a bad deal with three hotties.

So your $120 plus $40 for each girl was for the room and full service for three girls. That is $240 for the hour. All-inclusive. Steep, but sounds about right. So enjoy it! Then the girls ask for another $360? They will not take advantage of you if you are familiar with the pricing structures. If management there knew the girls charged an extra $360, the girls would be in trouble. Then they wanted a tip afterwards? And one bitch was watching TV? I like Luxor but that is not right. I will try to get Mic's money back for his next trip when I go there next time.

The first night at Mermaids, girls were paid at $80 each for them. Plus $20. That biatch Erica rewarded you by hitting below the belt: she told you five more minutes when my guess is that you were in the room for 20 minutes. She wants to rip you off in both time and money. Not good.

I had the same thing happen with me. What I learned from this is to not ever tip ahead of time but hold out the tip for afterwards. YMMV.

But Erica has lost my business as I was eyeing her in the past. Always wear your watch. You get 60 minutes. I also learned this the hard way. Twice. So I know this through my mistakes.

I was with Jasmine twice. Once for $100 and once a little lower. That included the cost of the room. The house makes money on the room. If you cannot agree with the girl on pricing she gets in trouble. Especially if it is a standard offer. Plus she makes no money. They do not go up often.

I am not trying to burst anyone's bubble. Someone else out there could be reading this and they will learn about the pricing. People shy away from MPs for the reason of not understand the pricing. I, too, was intimidated at first. I just got burned by a girl at the same place that Mic went to. I humbly posted this under chica report. So I am not claiming to be an expert. But I am experienced.

The beauty of AB/CC is that you know the cost of the room and girl. The only surprise is when the cum boys all want a buck.

As to the MPs, if I appear mad at the pricing it is because I don't like to see mongers get overcharged. That is the beauty of this site.

Also for the new guys: guys at the corner don't know the best places. Stay away from them. Neither do the taxi drivers. They are paid by tips by the establishments. Read a posting by Burt on how the cops stopped him after giving the corner guy a buck to get lost.

Great reading, though. I was really entertained by the post. I even read it twice.

Gekko: Choi, we all complain about loose pussy, but you complain the most. Ever think that your package may not be up to snuff?

LordNero: True, Gekko! We talked about this same thing in the alley last time. Doc, you can always try using a pump!

DrChoi: Let's see, I mention Giesel at AB has a loose pussy, someone says no.

I mention Diana of Mini has medium loose pussy, even then I cum twice in a session

Gekko did her few days later, and he said she was good.

Amigos, those two chicas have been around for very long time. They've fucked way more guys then you two guys have fucked putas combined.

Loose pussy is common in TJ… just some guys are less sensitive.

Sex in the City

ASIANMOVIELOVER

I had a good time last night. Arrived at 8pm with a buddy of mine. I'd been to TJ before, but in the afternoon and alone. My friend has never been in TJ.

We check out Hong Kong. There was a lot of dancing, but the strip show hadn't started. We hung out for a couple of minutes and saw nothing of interest so we headed over to AB.

I noticed a bunch of people were just outside of AB. Thought it must be crowded, so I told my friend we'll go to CC instead. Later on, I realized those people were there to just check out the girls as they come down from doing their business. A funny remark from one of those guys to a chica was "How was it?" as she was coming down the stairs.

At CC, we sat in one of those booths. A lot of girls, some were hot. Girls hang out at one side of the club, guys hang out on the other side. Not like AB, with those pushy girls that come up and ask you to buy them a drink.

Anyways, my friend spots a hottie by the door. But chicken that he was, I had to go to her to invite her over. She had on a red dress, 5'5", at least a C cup, face okay, body is medium hourglass shape, 7 on my scale. I directed her to sit with my friend and order her up a drink. We chat a little—actually very little because she doesn't speak English, nor do we speak Spanish.

I told me friend to fondle her tits. And I also give a couple of good squeezes. Let me tell you something, Mexican tits are the finest in the Americas. I ask my friend if he wants to do the girl. He says no, so I told him to wait for me in the club. I offer $50 to the girl and up we go. Upstairs, she demands the money first, so I said okay. Did the deed, CBJ… cowgirl… mish… doggie… cum… nothing out of the ordinary.

I met my friend back downstairs and ask him if he is going to do any of the girls. Said no because he wants to have lap dances only. I said okay then. Thought it to be kinda of a waste to go to TJ and not fuck any chica. But if he isn't up for it, I won't push it.

So off we went back to Hong Kong, hoping the strip show has started. I noticed the street where AB is was not that crowded, but the alley was crowded. We get to Hong Kong and they had started the shows.

We sat down for some drinks and watched the show. Saw a hot girl that I liked as she was gyrating on the bar, and asked her for a lap dance. Small, built body, but larger boobs, 8 on my scale. She gets off the bar and we enter this booth. Apparently the waiter is also a booth monitor and also a translator, as the girl doesn't speak English. So it was 20 dollars for two songs. When the song started, I did a little soft ass spanking, and the girl stopped and complained that I was spanking her. I said her butt was nice. She kept complaining. I thought to myself that this was not going to be a good dance. So she keeps dancing and gyrated her butt on me. I sucked her tits and humped her as she humped me until the two songs are up.

I was going to ask her to do a CBJ but being the complainer that she was, I didn't want her to suck my dick. It actually ruined everything. When I was fondling her all over, I noticed she had some lotion all over her body. Can anyone tell me what's up with that?

Anyway, I get out from the lap dance and my friend was sitting there with his drink. So I ask if he was going to go with any of these girls. He says no and wants to check out somewhere else.

So we got in a taxi and head for Beverly Hills. The driver was a dickhead. First, I tell him to go to Beverly Hills and he says he doesn't know where it is. So I tell him to use his radio to ask them for directions. He says the radio doesn't work, when in fact I hear people talking back a forth on the radio. Then he tells me there is another club, Lord Black. I was going to yell at him and say, "We don't want to go to fucking Lord Black!"

But with us being in a foreign country, I didn't say that. He kept insisting. So I told him to drop us off at 3rd and Revolución. When we get there, I just give him 5 bucks.

But he has the nerve to ask for a tip. "Fuck you. You didn't find the place and now you want a tip?" is what I would say if I was in the States. But me and my friend just get out of the taxi and ignore him and walk over to Beverly Hills.

At Beverly Hills, there are a couple of guys in suits standing outside directing us in. Actually, I noticed all clubs on Revolución are like that. So we sit down and we watch the show while we drank.

There were a couple of things I noticed here. First, the waiters here are like pimp daddys. Every five minutes, the pimp daddys bring a chica by and ask if you want a companion (cost: a drink for the girl) or lap dancing ($20 for one, two, or three songs; depending who asks). Second, there was a second girl in the audience that was getting it on with the strippers. Unfortunately she wouldn't strip down for us to view her assets. But she was fat all over, so that was all right. Third, booths that are on the side have these see-through curtains.

After a while of being there, a pimp daddy brings by a chica for me. She didn't speak English, but she was a tall 5'9", braided hair, B cups, with a bikini. Definitely a 9 'cuz I love those leggy girls. So I bargain for $20 bucks for two songs. Get to the booth and the pimp daddy says the girl is giving a special: for an extra $30 bucks I get a BJ with the dance. I tried to bargain it for $15, but the girl refused. So I said never mind.

Some things worth mentioning with the lap dance I had: I did a lot of tit sucking. She had nice big protruding nipples. She did a lot of humping and even thrusting motions to me. She had her thong on but still allowed me to finger her pussy. I just had to cum when she gave me a dry hand job with some heavy humping. As soon as I came, I told her to stop. You just can't get what she did in the US places!

So with that deed done, I walk my damp pants over to my friend and told him I'm done for the day.

All of the sudden, my friend sees The Girl. The best in the joint. Like 19 years old, 5'4", B cups, totally hot. When she was on stage, she wouldn't let us suck her young supple tits. Wouldn't even let us touch those. She was a 10 in my book. So I said to my friend, "Do her for me." I should have waited it out for her, but, like I said, I was done and wasn't in the mood to get another dance.

My friend tries to bargain with her. She wanted $20 for one song. Actually, my friend offered $20 for three songs when the pimp daddy brought her by, but when he approached her it was suddenly $20 for only one. He refused and settled for the second best looking girl in the joint (his opinion). Got three songs for $20.

Things he told me about his dance: Didn't let him finger her. Offered $60 extra for a BJ.

And that was our trip.

COUPLE OF THINGS WORTH MENTIONING:

1. Revolución Ave is really busy at night time.
2. What's with the lotions HK girls put on, but BH girls don't?
3. Know where you're going, 'cuz the taxi will try to rip you off every chance they can get.
4. Everything is good with BH except those pimp daddys. (If I

want a lap dance I will ask, don't keep offering!)

5. In the zone, there are people that come into the bars to sell stuff (gums, flowers, pictures with chicas…)

6. When you see the girls on Revo selling gum or whatever, buy some stuff from them. I feel bad because 75% of the time those girls will become hookers. And I don't think they have the intentions of being hookers when they grow up.

Did Grandma Ever Take it Up the Ass? Ask Grandpa!

AMO

How sick are you that you would even want to know? Jajaja!

I hit AB Thursday night at 4am. I had been thinking about doing Alejandra (Smith) all week and was glad to see her available.

I ask you, where else can you go into a bar, see a hot chick, and within 10-15 minutes be fucking her? She's always got a sucker in her mouth, so I brought her a lollipop shaped like a dick complete with a tiny condom. She laughed and showed it to a bunch of her amigas as we sat for a drink. We flirted a bit, and then went upstairs. I had always admired her body, but when she peeled off her dress, I fell to my knees and thanked God for having a cock!

She's got to have the biggest tits on a woman I've done so far in five years+ of TJ mongering. Like small honeydew melons that she kept rubbing in my face. She peeled off her thong next and started grinding a perfect ass on my rapidly growing dick... man, what a body!

Great covered BJ (I brought a chocolate condom). She really knows how to deep throat! After several minutes of an exquisite BJ, I sat up and told her it was her turn, but she said no, she didn't know me well enough yet.

I played with her pussy for a few minutes and we changed

rubbers to start the main event. Mish, reverse CG, her on top, and doggie. I loved it all!

I had paid for an hour and the knock came in 20 minutes!!! She didn't say anything and I'm thinking *uh-oh*. But then I realized she didn't say anything was because she was gasping with pleasure. A couple of times, she'd stop when we changed positions and would go back to deep throating for a couple minutes. She kept telling me, "Hmmm, muy grande!" I laughed and told her it was because of her. (Actually it was the Levitra, amazing!)

Finally finished, and she cleaned up at the sink, gave me a quick kiss, and split. Great session (really, all my sessions are 'cuz I'm a great lover!) I think with a couple repeats and increased confidence, we could make beautiful music together.

I did notice on my way out of the bar with Smith that AnaMaria was working. All reports I've read say that she's an afternoon chica, but both times I've seen her, it's been pretty late. She caught my eye and smiled. There's something about her that stirs my imagination (she's got tits and a pussy?) I guess I'm gonna have to find out what she's like and report back.

Next day, I went looking for fireworks (literally). Porfiro, the CC cabbie, had given me an address on Revo, yet the guy there said they didn't have any. But then he walked me over to another place called Adis Place; it's in a mini-mall on Revo between 5 and 6th. As I was walking down Revo, a guy kept trying to sell me everything/anything—jewelry, meds, and then finally said, "How about my sister?"

I laughed and asked, "How old?"

When he said 18, I said no thanks!

That night, I took my business partner to HK. We both had chicas we wanted to find, and although he lives with an AB chica, she wasn't working that night, so he felt safe in going. I wanted Darlene. She had fired me up a few weeks ago, but the waiter said she wasn't working. My buddy wanted Yasmine, but she was occupied with a monger who kept her busy all night when she wasn't dancing. We hung out for awhile and decided to bail to CC.

We lucked out in CC, found a booth right next to the dance floor, and grabbed a couple cold ones. I asked for "lager" from the bartender. He served up two Tecates, but amazingly enough, gave us Dos XX when I asked for them instead, no hassle.

Most of the chicas were so-so, but at one point a very hot dancer came on, and I noticed that all of us had gotten dollars out to give her!. I saw Beatrice and happily ignored her. She kept positioning herself in my line of vision, and even grabbed some guy's hand to walk by me, but I couldn't care less. It's over for me.

Leaving the bar later, I tossed the keys to my amigo. I told him, "Hey, if we get stopped, you're Mexican. It's gonna be less of a hassle than if I'm driving."

Sure as shit, at the end of the Rapida, where you can either get in line to border cross or go towards Zona Rio, there was a blockade. Flashlight shined, pulled us over, and the cop asked my buddy if he had been drinking. He admitted two beers (*more like seven or eight*), and the cop asked who owned the car. I said it was mine, and my friend was driving because I had drank more, so he was driving. The cop told my friend to get out and I got out as well, but he advised me to get back in.

Afterwards, my buddy said the cop told him he could fine him for even drinking at all, to which he replied "Go ahead," and the cop realized he wasn't going to get any bribes from us, and let us go. I may or may not have been able to pull that off myself, but glad I didn't have to find out. The cop did have him blow in his face (I really wanted to see the rolled up cone "Breathalyzer") but the cop decided he wasn't drunk. So off we went towards home after another fine night in the Zona.

Good and Bad Report

BUTTMAN

Went back to Adelita on Friday about 11pm. There were a lot of guys hanging outside the bar waiting for the girls to come down. I had read about that sort of thing but I've never seen that many guys doing it. IT WAS PACKED AND HOT inside. Less American music than the previous night and more local music.

I did find they are now selling big sealed bottles of water for $4. WELL WORTH IT! It is packaged by Coke. You can take your drinks you buy in the club upstairs and back into the club after you come back down.

There were many more women than on Thursday, but still the quality of the women seemed better last December and January than now. Had a good session with a short okay-looking cute chica with dimples that had a great attitude. She had on black pants and a striped shirt. She was very friendly downstairs. I don't remember her name but had a great time.

Then we went to Lord Black for a while where I hung out with Sofia who used to work at Madonna's about two years ago. Lord Black is the top of the line 'pricey' USA-style strip club in TJ. Mostly USA music all night. A/C was pumping. Cover charge was $8 and the "walk-away" did not bring the price down any for us. Very professionally run club. You get a receipt with every drink purchase. Free 'hot as hell' peanuts to eat. Awesome lights on the stage. They were playing a bootleg copy of *Bad Boys 2* on a TV also.

So about Sofia. She is tall… long dark hair… big natural tits… very nice. The private dances at LB are upstairs. I think $20 per song. They don't cut the songs short, but still… $20 for a lap dance is a bit steep with Adelita around the corner. Mileage varies depending on the chica but I have never had anything but a good grinding and a bit of hand action there. Sofia did about smother me with her tits though. My friend got a private dance from a VERY MUSCULAR chica. Kind of like a mini-Chyna from the old WWF days. She was hard as a rock with no fat anywhere. I told him he better take a dance from her or risk getting his ass kicked.

Then back to Adelita we went—via cab, of course—where we saw something rare. A group of working chicas was on the dance floor (all wearing cowboy hats) western line dancing to Latin versions of US country music songs… like *Achy Breaky Heart*. It was part comedy and part turn on…

Anyway, one of the girls dancing was VERY CUTE/PRETTY with tattoos (line art above on small of her back, black panther on her back between her shoulders, and the METALLICA logo below her belly button) and piercings on her belly button, eyebrow, and tongue. Her name is Blue and she had on a two-piece blue skirt/top outfit.

Now let me tell you… I thought the stars were lined up PERFECTLY for me! My favorite color is blue. My favorite NFL team is the Panthers. I love heavy metal music. I dig tattoos and piercings on chicks. I've been dying for a BJ from a chica with a tongue ring, so as you can imagine, I thought I was set for the night!

Well, let me tell you something… IF YOU ARE THINKING OF HOOKING UP WITH BLUE… DO NOT DO IT!

She seemed nice downstairs, but once upstairs she wanted the money up front then… well, let me put it to you like this: a corpse would have been more lively.

It was the worst roll in the hay I've ever had in my life! Very boring… just laid there. NO BJ AT ALL!!! Two lifeless positions. No way possible to even think about a finish. Told her to hit the road after only 10 minutes! To top it all off, it was like a sauna in that room! I took one for the team to pass along this info to everyone here.

So the lesson to be learned here is choose one with a great attitude more so than looks and you'll probably be much happier. I've found the more frisky they are downstairs, the more you get upstairs overall. If they are at all standoffish (not touching you at all) or business-like downstairs, then save your money and time.

Later on, I saw a new chica in Adelita, a DAMN HOT one in my book. Young girl goes by Samantha with long bleach blonde curly hair. Tight jeans. She could pass for an American except she doesn't speak English. Wearing a half-jersey style shirt that said FOXY 69 on the front. Anyone with info on her? She blew off my friend when he tried to hook up with her.

And why did they bother to put in A/C or heat vents in the rooms above Adelita if they are not going to turn on the damn A/C blowers?

Back to the border about 4am with no line or wait to get back to the US but they had the walk-over closed! THE BASTARDS! Why are they closing it? We had to walk all the way around San Ysidro to get back to the place we always (up to now) have parked. I think we'll park on the west side of the highway tomorrow, a much shorter walk if the crossover is closed.

Fear & Self-Loathing in Tijuana

Matiz

I feel an obligation to tell Flor's story. Perhaps it's because, over time, I've come to realize that I've helped in some small way to create Flor and so bear some responsibility for who she is now. Just as in seeking out the chicas of Tijuana to satisfy our desires, we all share some responsibility for creating the Flors of the world.

I first met her about five years ago when she was a dancer in a Revo bar. She was a lusty, slutty, raven-haired Mexicana and I just had to have her right then. The only private space was in the manager's office. So she led me back there and, captivated by her tight dancer's ass, silicone D-cups, and slutty appearance, I bent her over the manager's couch, pulled aside her thong, and did her quickly.

The next time I saw her, about a year later, Flor was resplendent in knee-high black boots, thigh-high mesh stockings, and a two-piece fake leopard skin outfit. The top was cut very low in the front to show maximum cleavage, while the bottom was cut very high in the back to show maximum cheek-age.

Making small talk for the first time with her, I learned that Flor was trying to support five—count 'em, five—kids. She produced pictures of her "bebes" from her purse. Several of the kids were actually in their late teens. The daughters looked exactly like mom, only younger. It was a little strange to talk about her kids while she was massaging Pancho and I was playing with mom's large boobies. "No condóns," she said wistfully. "Accidentes."

The Pope would be proud, I thought.

Upstairs, we had another fine session that rated pretty high on the Nasty Meter. Afterward, we made more small talk as she sat on the side of the bed and brushed her hair. I asked her about the transvestite floorshow in the bar in the evenings. Had she seen it? Was it any good?

"Oh, yes, it's good. But they charge a $5 cover."

"Really?"

"Yes", she says, her voice getting sarcastic, "They're artists, you know."

"Well," I said, "You're an artist, too, a dancer."

"No, I'm a fucking bitch," she replied.

When I looked surprised, she explained that she had complained to the manager that the TVs got $20 for dancing while she only got $2 for a half-hour of grinding away and letting guys grope her.

She said that the manager told her, "They're artists. You're just a fucking bitch, a whore. You have a pussy and your only function is to service men with your pussy."

There was a mix of anger and sadness in her expression, and I sensed she was frustrated to the point of tears. With eyes watering, she concluded, "I guess when you have a pussy, you're a bitchita, a fucking whore. When you don't have a pussy, you're an artist."

I sat down next to her and put my arm around her.

I told her that, to me, she was a true "artiste" and that she made me feel very good whenever I was with her. What the manager had said was cruel and heartless. I couldn't help but feel empathy for her.

The next time I ran into her, many months later, she looked as sexy as ever, but seemed to have become more erratic and sordid in her behavior. In the room, she confided that she had a "fantasia." *Que fantasia?* She wanted me to slap her in the face, call her a whore, and tell her, "Suck my cock, you bitch." And when she did, I was supposed to grab her hair and tell her, "Suck harder, puta!" In perrito, I should slap her hard on the ass and demand, "Fuck me, bitch. Harder. Deeper."

So I played the dominant role, although a little halfheartedly, not wanting to actually hurt her. Several times she told me to slap her harder, and in the end, I got "in the spirit" of the moment and played my role pretty well. When I completed the obligatory facial finish, she got up from the bed, various bodily fluids dripping from her face and breasts, and she slowly wiped herself with a tissue.

She started chuckling, and then laughing. I joined in. Soon we were both roaring with laughter. My laughter was my relief that this really was just play-acting.

Hers? Quien sabe? Had she seen this in a porn movie? Had other customers demanded that she act this way? Could she possibly enjoy it? Was she becoming crazy or even self-destructive?

Perhaps a year went by before I saw Flor again. She remembered me but seemed to have progressed further into her "fantasias". This time, she said, she wanted to do a threesome with another woman. Not, it turns out, for the other woman to join in, but just so she could just lie there and watch enviously as Flor and I enjoyed ourselves.

So as we had sex, Flor demonstrated how the fantasy would work. Every so often, she would turn to our imaginary playmate and say, "He's fucking me now, bitch. He isn't going to fuck you because your pussy's smelly. You just watch, bitch." Throughout our session, she continued to play out this fantasy, often turning to "her" and saying, "See? You're not worth fucking. He wants to fuck me, not you."

Did I think this was a little weird? Of course. Was it weirder than other things I've experienced in TJ? Hard to say.

But I got the feeling that over the several years I'd been seeing her, Flor was moving in a downward trajectory toward some kind of unknown sexual place that was filled with her own fear, anguish, and self-loathing. Someone I had first known as just a lusty, energetic, erotic sex-worker was morphing into something dark and compulsive that I couldn't really understand. My first thought was drugs. But her coworkers insisted she was clean and I never saw any evidence of drug use. Just her increasingly strange sexual preferences.

As I think about my experiences with Flor, I am reminded of Kurt Vonnegut's insightful comment: You are what you pretend to be. Therefore, be very careful what you pretend to be.

Without starting a philosophical debate about the nature of reality, let me just say that on some level, Vonnegut is correct. Actions do have a transforming effect on people. A "good" person who constantly acts rude, selfish, and mean-spirited will eventually become callous and unpleasant. And a mean-spirited person who repeatedly shows kindness and generosity to others will eventually become less unpleasant and more likeable. Over time, our actions shape us like the rushing water in a river wears down the sharp rocks.

So what does that mean for the ladies of Tijuana, who spend their entire careers pretending to be someone else—with their "stage names," false bios, faked orgasms, feigned affection for clients, and faux sluttishness? If a woman pretends long enough, eventually she begins to take on some of the characteristics of the "persona" she projects to others. She tries so hard to be the whore that eventually it's hard for her to distinguish the "pretend" whore from the "real" woman.

In the end, of course, she is just trying to be what she thinks we mongers want her to be—wanton, alluring, available, accommodating, insatiable. Does she really "want" me to come on her face? Does she really "want" to be slapped? Does she really "want" to be in a threesome with another woman? Does she really "want" to be treated like trash?

At first, probably not. But if she keeps acting the part of a worthless cum receptacle, she eventually will become a worthless cum receptacle, at least in her own eyes. Fear and self-loathing. And, however small, I had a hand in helping her develop that self-image.

Last weekend, I unexpectedly ran into Flor again, this time in a popular Zona Norte bar. She still maintains her dancer's figure, she still has the large, artificial D-cups, and she is still as predatory and erratic as ever. Her first words to me as she sat down were, "I want you to fuck me in my mouth, my pussy, and my ass." Then she licked her lips slowly with her tongue and gave me a leering look.

When we got to the room, she told me, "I no like condom. Joo fuck me without condom, sí?" I demurred, but she complained, "I want a baby with joo. Joo no want baby with me?"

Her words were like a well-lit highway sign on the road to Hell that says, "You are almost there." Five children to care for and she's now offering me unprotected sex.

She had certainly come a long way in five years; from the slightly tarty dancer I'd bent over the manager's sofa to this pornographic caricature of a prostitute. As Vonnegut might say, she had now become exactly what she had pretended to be all these years—a whore.

Whatever part of the "real" Flor that had existed before—the woman, the friend, the mother—was now inextricably bound together with the whore. I know this happens all the time in TJ. But usually it's more gradual and less obvious. And usually I don't have a front row seat when it's happening.

I said I wanted to tell Flor's story because, on some level, we all have a role in creating the Flors of TJ with our desires and our sexual demands. True, it may only be a small part that we play, given the hundreds, or thousands, of customers a woman like Flor has had over the years. But I am a thread in the tapestry of Flor's life and contribute to its mosaic. And so in telling her story I am also telling my story. I, too, am what I pretend to be.

I ordered her to get down on her knees and give me a blowjob. Then I put on a condom and fucked her in the ass. Then I came on her face. She smiled after I finished and kissed me on the lips. She was very happy with the propina I gave her for her services, but dressed quickly and rushed back to the bar hoping to find another customer before her shift ended.

It's the aspect of TJ I find most unseemly and unattractive: woman as mindless sexual object; man—myself—as mindless Priapus. I'd like to think I'm so much more than that, but you are what you pretend to be. And if the shoe fits…

I certainly don't write this to judge Flor. In truth, I like her. She's just doing what she believes she needs to do to help herself and her kids.

And I'm not judging our hobby, nor the other ladies in TJ, nor any of you. I have no right to judge and no interest in judging. It's unproductive and leads nowhere.

But as an observer, I am struck by the many subtle effects that we—customers and providers—have on each other. Every encounter we have with a chica in TJ, no matter how fleeting it is, affects us and the chicas in subtle ways we can't see or even imagine. Over time, the cumulative effect of all these experiences is inevitably to transform each of us. Just as Flor was transformed. Just as I have been transformed.

I don't know what any of it means from a larger perspective. Increasingly, I'm astounded at my own ignorance. As a young man, I thought I knew something, but over the years, I've come to accept that the sum total of all my "wisdom" is just a tiny speck floating in a vast ocean of ignorance.

I have no answers, no remedies, no suggestions.

But I do believe Socrates was correct that "…the unexamined life is not worth living." So I pose the question. Food for thought, if you will, for some idle moment you might have away from TJ and las mujeres. Sometimes, just asking the right question can point us in a new, and perhaps better, direction.

Amigo Commentary

JD: Great post. Some of my favorite reading on this site as always… thanks for sharing. The only part I disagreed with was the gradual part… you got to see her decline over several years. I think this is actually a pretty good length of time and more gradual than most. Most of the declines/changes in chicas that I have seen have occurred in months or 1-2 years.

I remember when Mary Louisa (SG now at HK) was scared, nervous, and shy.

Three months later she was acting like Cascades' finest stuck up biatch.

I remember Kenia de CC right around the time she first hooked up with her padrote… she was kind, sweet, and couldn't play a fiddle.

Today, she still is kind and sweet but she plays more fiddles than fiddlers and is good enough at it that she could beat a polygraph.

While I thoroughly enjoy the Zona, I never underestimate the impact time and people within it affect the chicas and the mongers.

CountryJohn: Thank you for posting this thoughtful, observant post. I just want to comment that the first step in understanding something is a clear and unobstructed view of the component parts.

You answered your own questions several times in your own post but you keep asking them.

I suggest you re-read your post. The answers lie within.

In the end, the very thing that she resisted, she became. Funny how the real world works, eh?

Rosinate: What a well-written story of a person's plight.

A person who thinks or is told enough times that they can do better knows better than to work in this industry. Albeit, there are a few such as the famous Tania who has kept it together, saved a very large amount of money, and bought land and houses. But the Tanias of the industry are few and far between, and quite the exception.

The story of Flor is more the norm: the spiral down the path of what she thinks is right or what she wants. But really, so much of what happened is brought on by her environment of growing up.

Nose: Thanks for sharing. Brilliant stuff.

And what about us?

What kind of people do we become?

What effect have my behavior patterns had on me?

Remember, too, that we judge others by their actions, but ourselves by our motivations.

If, say, John Smith slaps you in the face, you bristle in anger at him because he slapped you in the face. You might ask yourself, "Whatever impelled him to slap me, when I have only been his friend this entire time?"

But John remembers above all why he slapped you, not that he slapped you. He remembers his motivation, what provoked him. You remember mostly that he slapped you.

You might react by slapping him in turn, thinking to yourself: "It serves him right, the bastard slapped me!" You think of your motivation for slapping him, but he will mostly remember that after provoking him to slap you, you then slapped him, provoking him again, committing yet another injustice!

Ah, humanity! Ah, Bartelby!

— No se (y nunca sabia mucho tampoco)

PS: All food for thought, but don't let your actions make you become a person you don't want to be, and take care of your own and yourself, never letting a John Smith come within slapping distance of you!

MRight: If we are what we pretend to be, then we should pretend to be who we want to be.

CountryJohn: That's fucking deep, man. Consider this:
First of all, you ARE.
You decide what to BE.
Pretending is something you DO.
What you HAVE is the result.

AllanSmithy: The abusive sex part was a total turn on!

KCaveral: I have to wonder though; do you not believe that there are a small percentage of mongers who do treat the ladies as just that, ladies?
Yes, ultimately we fuck them, but can we not fuck them with care and tenderness and kindness? Or does that just make me a PLM because I do not treat them like a whore?

SenorPanocha: Of course you can, and it does not remotely make you anything like a PLM.

Maxximus: This post is why you should never go into the personal details of the whores you fuck. Don't ruin the fun by getting all personal.
She's a whore. You have money. Enough said…Next!
Fuck 'em and leave 'em…

Crip: Matiz, you said it yourself early in the story… when you first met her, "she was…lusty, slutty…" I'm not terribly convinced that she didn't find her present emotional longitude/latitude a decade or two before she became fortunate enough to make your acquaintance (I believe that she may be loose about condom use, but she isn't intentionally and actively inviting others to father a golden child for her). I know in your thesis that you're aware that you are a mere grain of sand in her metamorphosis and not literally a significant contributor. Neither was her boss who lined her up against the TV dancers; he just validated what she already felt.
It is ironic that I am particularly moved by it… not because you and I are friends and have explored and discussed the territory together, but instead because my last Zona moment last weekend literally paralleled yours, and I departed with a

black mood… the mood generated by my guilt about being part of a system that could destroy a young sweetheart so cruelly and summarily as my amiga whom we encountered at our last stop of the weekend's journey.

But in the case of my exposure to E's premature demise, it is much more about alcohol than sex for money. I first met her the afternoon that you and I renewed our acquaintance with this particular bar some months ago. It was early. She was sober, delightful, breezy, hopeful, and had boundaries.

Since then I've encountered her three more times and she is deeply lost—a habitual blackout drinker—a habit, of course, dictated by her work. I have desperately tried to reach her but she's blacked out with her eyes open, so it is impossible.

I am a nice guy but I've not habitually acted the part of Chief Save A Ho, yet I feel a need to seek her out again—EARLY—and talk to her… maybe more. I have been maintaining that the most destructive aspect of the trade in TJ is the drinking more than the whoring… in any event, it is a potent 1-2 physical/emotional combination.

Eric73: A deep and insightful post. But rest assured, for all the disasters in the Zona there are also thousands of success stories. Women who have done it for a while, raised the money needed, then gone off to bigger and better things. I can think of several chicas from HK and RR that have gone on to bigger and better in Mexico and the US. But the more years they have been in the business, the more difficult it is to get out. Change isn't always easy. And then bringing kids into the mix along with the useless fathers these chicas seem to pick… what a disaster.

GMO428: Whores or not, they are somebody's sister, somebody's daughter, somebody's loved one. They are real. Be kind, tip well, and above all, treat them with respect. We cannot save the world alone, but for a brief moment you can help brighten someone's day.

Darkness: You start off going to TJ to see what it is like. You fuck some hookers, then you get to know them, and you start to see them as more than just something you stick your dick in. The more you see them, the more you view them more than just a good fuck. It's easy to fall for a TJ girl, but it's hard to love them. Or maybe it's just because I am drunk out of my mind.

I don't know about you guys, but sometimes—well, just once maybe—I think I can "save" just one of them from the life they chose, but in the end, maybe it's "us" that need to be saved more than them…

TJBone: Some of us just prefer doing pretty girls half our age (or less) instead of what's available to us on this side. Sure, it's superficial and artificial but the little head wants what it wants and will make us miserable if it doesn't get it.

Pew: I am moved by all of this, but unable to write all I'm thinking. Perhaps I can write some of my thoughts later.

But your post and the quote from Kurt Vonnegut "You are what you pretend to be. Therefore, be very careful what you pretend to be," are memorable and will be with me from now on.

I posted a day or so ago my thanks for TJA. This is one more piece of evidence why this has become a part of my life.

Edgar: Re-reading this amazing post, I'm struck by the verbal abuse by the boss as the turning point. I've been involved with a Mexican woman who is in an unhappy marriage and have noticed the verbal bludgeoning this very strong woman takes from her husband. I think it's an extension of the battered-women stereotype in Mexico (i.e., that physical violence happens all the time, especially in the working class), but by means of words from a man in a power position. Then the victim hardens and wants to abuse the next person.

TJFlyer: Matiz - wow! Your post was one of the most interesting and deep tales to appear on the pages of TJA in a long, long time.

It does read as a very sad tale. Of a woman and a mother trying her best to raise five kids in a third world country by practicing the world's oldest profession... The lifestyle has to have an effect on these women, just as being a cop or an ambulance driver or social worker has an effect on those persons.

I recently found myself starting to entertain PLM thoughts over a chica I have been fucking for the past year. What shook me out of this was reading other posts about this same chica and my fellow mongers' experiences with her. Seemed very similar to my sessions, and here I thought I was "special".

Last week I when I last saw her, she was busy with another client, and I observed her in action in the bar. I realized that TJ is truly a place for most of us to get away to, have a good time lifting drinks with buddies and getting some strange pussy. Not a place to get into a PLM relationship with a prostitute...

Sometimes in TJ—in fact, most times—it's best not to lose sight of this reality. It just sobers you to think how fucked most of the sex workers in the Zona Norte have it... makes you really appreciate being able to cross back into the USA and return to our normal lives... something many folks in TJ would trade an arm and a leg for...

Ryu: *TJFlyer wrote, "I realized that TJ is truly a place for most of us to get away to, have a good time lifting drinks with buddies and getting some strange pussy."*

That's the problem most guys don't see, they are only there for strange whereas this is for most girls, their lives. To me, it's kind of like being in a war zone; it changes you while you're there and even afterwards you have the after-war syndrome. A guy who wants the perfect GF not just outside but also inside is invariably going to be upset as these girls are far from perfect inside. Most are pretty messed up especially while working. The sad thing is that most guys want the perfect girl. I mean, who doesn't? Right?

And in many ways that's what you get most of the time with the Zona girls when you are paying and paying big. You have a gorgeous girl in your arms, you get great sex, and she listens to you and treats you like a real man. But it's when their real self comes out—the good and the bad—that guys say, "Man, she's not perfect. Fuck that! If I wanted imperfect, I'd find a US girl." I call this the Falling in Love With [club name] Not With [real name] Syndrome.

And it's this unreasonable expectation from a lot of mongers that cost guys a lot of money and ruin some of the girls' lives. It's really in everyone's best interest for mongers to just come and fuck and for working girls to just keep their distance. But of course, many single guys want more, first friendship and then romance, and that's when people's lives get fucked up.

TJTaxi: Nice post Ryu, and pretty much on the money.

The problem with most guys that visit the Zona is that they have no real social skills (or so they think) to deal with a stateside relationship. It is equally difficult for the "working" chicas, as most are "working" because of low self-esteem.

The guys come down to find that they are "loved" and "wanted" by almost all the girls they come in contact with. Confidence builds and they now feel like "something special" instead of Joe Blow.

The girls (for the most part) feel "special", as they are showered with affection, admiration, and respect that most likely was never given them by family or ex-spouses.

The sad part is that these two types of dependent personalities very rarely can coexist.

Matiz: Erip, as you well know, I don't lose sleep at night worrying about the chicas in TJ. They make their own decisions in life, as we all do, and they have to live by the consequences of those decisions. Flor, not me, chose to have five kids. She chose to work as a prostitute. She continues to make the decisions about what she will do, with whom, and for how much. I'm just a very small comet orbiting in and out of her solar system every so often.

The responsibility I was referring to was really more of that abstract responsibility that we all feel toward our fellow men and women, the natural human sense of empathy for others that we feel in the midst of their difficulties and despair. If we affect the person we smile at in the elevator or the Indian lady on Revolución to whom we toss a dollar or the drunk in the bar for whom we call a cab—if we have some small impact on the lives of total strangers, then how much more so do we influence—and are influenced by—the chicas with whom we have intimate sex?

In the end, though, the extent to which we choose to become our brother's keeper is a decision each of us has to make for ourselves. I learned a long time ago that I can't control what others do or the decision they make, and I certainly shouldn't tie my own happiness to what others do or don't do. Wrestling with the very human empathy we feel towards las chicas while at the same time recognizing the inevitability of their frequently downward trajectories in life is a common pastime among those of us who visit TJ with any consistency. It was in that spirit that I wrote this report, trying, yet again, to fathom my own complexities, insecurities, and faults, and to put them into some kind of meaningful perspective.

CRIP: Matiz... perfect! And besides if those of us who are "wrestling with the very human empathy we feel towards las chicas" choose to stay away, we just leave the ladies to the exclusive use of those without empathy. That wouldn't help to moderate those downward trajectories, would it?

I somewhat disagree with your statements regarding the chicas being responsible for their own bad decisions—good liberal as I am I have to give consideration to bad decisions made by those innocently ignorant and operating under economic and social coercion.

I have at times attempted to dispense patriarchal wisdom to the young ones in particular—they genuinely appreciate my good intentions but the blankness in their eyes can be blinding. Then I start behaving like Jerry Lewis at his most childish again and they are filled with delight.

X-Wiz: *TJTaxi wrote, "The problem with most guys that visit the Zona, is that they have no real social skills (or so they think) to deal with a stateside relationship."*

I am not too sure about that. Most of guys I know who frequent the Zona are also very adventurous and sociable people stateside. It takes a certain personality to be able to get naked and fuck a complete stranger few minutes after meeting her. The high social skills may be the reason why their relationships often fail. They like to keep meeting new people, thus the more chance of having affairs, etc.

Irishman: The Wiz is usually correct in his posts, but here I must respectfully disagree. Let's not kid ourselves; going to the Zona regularly often is a sign of having significant issues. It ain't normal behavior. Most (I said *most, not all*) guys who visit the Zona with regularity are dysfunctional people with significant negative traits of one kind or another, often poor social skills, physical appearance issues, substance abuse issues, maturity issues, personal relationship issues, etc., etc.

People who are functioning well and have healthy and successful personal relationships are usually not the people who frequent the Zona.

Walk into AB on a Friday or Saturday night and often you will think you have accidentally walked into a convention of nerds and losers.

X-Wiz: Who decides that being a nerd is a bad thing? What is your definition of a loser? By the way, have you gone to Comic-Con before? The more nerdy/loser looking the guy is, the more hot girls he gets. If you show a picture of Quentin Tarantino to a gal who knows nothing about him, she may think he's a truly ugly and loser. Yet he gets to bang Uma Thurman and many other hotties.

IRISHMAN: Well, Wiz, I am not sure I can define it, but I know one when I see one. As to Comic-Con, I haven't been, but based on what you say I am definitely going next year!

X-WIZ: Sounds like the congressman telling the artist that he cannot define what is considered pornographic but knows it when he sees it.

Actually, I do agree that there are some losers in the Zona. They are easy to spot because they do not treat chicas very well. At least that's my definition of a loser.

MASTERMONGER: As usual, I agree with most everything Irishman is saying. As a group, mongers sure are fucked up just as bad as the putas and even worse at times. I believe every time you visit Tijuana, you lose a little bit of your sanity, and if you go everyday, you're one LUCKY SON OF A BITCH, but in the END, your 'wienie' and your 'BRAIN' are going to be FRIED!!!!

Where I differ from Irishman is that I believe a healthy and successful guy can visit the Zona, cheat on his wife and/girlfriend, and not suffer any ill effects. All of us have our 'dark side' and we need to let him out every so often to have fun. So in the Zona you'll find like Irishman says: nerds, losers, and YES, even a few WINNERS—just not too many.

But really, it doesn't matter, because we can all have FUN, just as long as the 'dysfunction' allows you to work and make money, because in Tijuana you don't need any 'social skills', just a few bucks.

JD: I think that in a sense both the monger and the chica need to be saved. That's usually why the sex and lust turn into something so much more so fast. When you take two people with issues and feelings of loneliness and misunderstandness and put them together, it forms a quick bond. In a way, they understand each other. However, neither one of them is suited to bring the other one out of the hole that they are in. They are comforted by the fact that they have something in common and an understanding, but they are also shackled by what they have in common at the same time.

It's like taking two heroin addicts and sticking them together to try to get clean… while they understand each other and bond because of it, they don't try to get each other clean; they sink deeper into the issues that brought them together in the first place.

Amo: Practice random acts of kindness. The good you do comes back to you.

Pew: If there were no laws or morality involved in the profession, they would be heroines and highly respected. (Have you ever seen a severely handicapped man in the zone with a lady? I have. There is more than money involved there.)

I don't have any answers. If I were king, there would be no need for the profession. Or I would make it an honorable calling, well paid and there if someone wanted or needed it. But that's not going to happen.

Until then, there are only thoughts and many unanswered questions.

JoeCougar: There is another facet of this jewel of a thread, although perhaps a bit shallow, but did it occur to the original poster that the girls are basically actresses and that they become better actresses as time goes by learning what men want to hear and do so as to earn more money?

I'm sure there is some truth to the "you become what you pretend" theory, but more likely when she is done wiping the cum off her face and pocketing your money, she goes home to her esposo and niños, watches TV, does the dishes, and goes out with her family to spend your money.

Sure, some girls go down the swirling drain of degradation, but others are professionals and just keep getting better at earning $$$. Either way, I wouldn't worry too much about it. It's been going on for thousands of years.

Like a Virgin, Yo!

CRIP

I am suffering post-monger overindulgence syndrome this week after spending a vacation running around TJ, Ensenada, and Tecate last week. I can't get it together enough to put together the comprehensive trip report that I'd hoped would be my contribution to this site. So what follows is THE highlight of all time, plus a few other great moments. Sorry that my first report will have to omit the name of the key player, but the necessity of that will become obvious.

I arrived in TJ on Monday and remained until Wednesday night. Thursday day, I enjoyed in Ensenada with a long time amiga con derechos, then back to TJ for Thursday night.

Monday night at CC was as dead as I've ever seen this club, night or day. I was greeted by a small posse of regular meseros. While I chewed the fat with them, I noted a potent siren smile aimed my way from a petite brown-skinned young adorable from a few tables away. She just fixed it on me and I couldn't help feeling the weight of it. I goofily kept checking intermittently hoping to have an unobserved moment of assessing assets other than her smile—resulting in the continuous embarrassment of being caught in her headlights. No cool going on here. Why should she ever avert her billboard smile since I'm essentially the only free agent customer in the joint? She was locked on.

However, my attention was diverted by a half dozen of CC's most noted party girls sitting in the big booths with a couple of trolls buying fichas for all. When the DJ fired up this year's number one TJ bar hit, "Gasolina", party central chica Marbel dragged the whole lot on to the dance floor for some amusing and sexy dance floor games. So I had something to distract me from regular glances to the siren, but when I did remember to glance, she caught me almost every time.

Tuesday night, I am in CC with an amigo and the place is actually functioning with a commercially viable count of chicas and customers. The siren is on premises and we pick up where we left off... me stealing glances, her catching all of them with her outsized smile, including during periods when she was con ficha con otro baboso. This was getting almost spooky.

Why didn't I approach her by now? Hey, that's a good question. The answer is a change in career 18 months ago forced me back into "weekend warrior" status in TJ. I don't want to go near AB on weekend nights. This was Tuesday, and CC was only a meeting place. My amigo and I wanted to sit in AB (of all places) for a spell... just because it was Tuesday and such a thing would be possible. So we were off to AB... not yet time to answer the siren's smiles.

Following a dynamite session with a Playboy Centerfold at AB named Mariana, I was spent and my amigo was headed for home. I went back to CC where I had the pleasure of commiserating with a number of long time amigas, but not free from the continuous smiling gaze of the siren. At this point, she is no doubt beginning to think there may be something wrong (*GAY*) about me.

Well, what she doesn't know is where I've been and the leche and dinero already contributed in other corners of the Zona. Just as I talk myself into at least an initial "marinating" ficha or two with the siren, she's out the door—two-piece pink miniskirt and halter top combo turned to blue jeans, sweatshirt, and baseball cap, her flowing black hair now a pony tail squeezed out of the back of the cap.

I return to TJ on Thursday after the 24-hour hiatus with the chica in Ensenada. Ensenada chica has enormous appetites and so I'm now back in CC seriously depleted in all ways that a human body can be depleted, but most especially used up in the libido department. I was again with my amigo from Tuesday night. We had another sit-down in AB during which I had a couple of drinks with one of the most attractive spinners I've ever encountered in TJ. Yadira de Acapulco, sort of a second coming of current AB spinner headliner Malena (aka Maria Magdalena), but IMO far more beautiful facially, and unlike Malena, STACKED, and naturally so!

Yadira's company served to replenish me to a good degree, but she would not realize the benefit of that because Thursday was my final opportunity to get with the siren since another trip to Ensenada was planned for the following day with no plan to return to TJ. I reluctantly said goodbye to Yadira and sincerely promised her a payday down the line.

'Round midnight, we were sitting in CC. My amigo quickly secured the most famous of all the CC legends, the magnificent Gabby. My siren sat with a young Carlos Santana lookalike at the bar about 15 feet beyond our table… and yes, continuing our festival of smiles even as this brown magic woman nursed non-alcoholic drinks with Carlos. Finally the moment arrives. Carlos kisses her on the cheek and moves out the door, and my amigo is having what he later reported as one of the great sessions of his life with Gabby (damn, I hope she hangs around for a few more months).

Then finally, I am sitting with the siren. All the delay and anticipation and mystery about to be redeemed. We most seriously enjoyed each other's company in the bar for about an hour. She portrays as a university graduate from a southern Mexico state and represents herself as having serious political aspirations. We had a lot to talk about in subject areas not usually tread upon in the booths of Chicago Club. She's against continuing toleration of prostitution in Mexico… jajaja! I love her but she's a regular Justice Clarence Thomas in the making (see affirmative action).

So though we held hands and by rote, I did a little bit of what I usually do to set a romantic tone preceding a session, our conversational focus was more on the liberal arts than the sensual arts. There was no way for me to gauge what I could expect from her in the room.

Once in the hotel, the mystery would instantly evaporate. The door closed and locked, we stood at the foot of the bed. I grizzly-bear embraced her, lowered my face to hers, and the two of us just snapped. She churned up a tidal wave of passion and initially, it was hard for me to keep up.

I was in a state of shock. This kind of intensity just doesn't materialize with las sexo servidoras, much less on a first encounter. When I finally broke through my seasoned cynicism and came to terms with the idea that she wasn't pretending, I ran quickly as I could to catch up to her and for the rest of the night, we were in lock step.

Let me say it clearly: this was the single most intense night of passion I have ever experienced with any sexual partner in my entire long life. Yes, I felt like a deflowered 53-year-old initiate. Makes me wonder if my life with women to now has been deficient. I hadn't thought so, or was it that I had just experienced something truly extraordinary: hitting the progressive jackpot at CC?

And yeah, this was my first bareback all the way adventure (excepting a couple of momentary surprises in dark caverns of Isis and other such depraved misadventures). Admittedly, I have been tempted over the last couple of years to drop my guard, but I have not, in fact, volunteered for BB sex with either a sex worker, TJ novia, or short-term hometown hookup for many a year.

In this instance, of course, it wasn't discussed yet I knew it was coming. Of course, there was no chance that I would interrupt the "flow" (no pun intended... geez!) of the clouds we were floating on for an introduction of something as repugnant as greased latex. This lovemaking felt like the composition of a sensual symphony and the use of a condom would have struck a harshly dissonant note.

At this point in any post shared among intelligent gentlemen comes rationalization. Well, despite appearances—this chica on the surface fits in with every other young, underfed, know-nothing 3rd world morena—she nevertheless holds herself out as an evolved "new Mexicana", educated, ambitious, independent (i.e. she's on the pill). And of course when the storm passed, she insisted on her own motion that the experience was as unique to her as it had been to me, and that she's never done bareback nuthin' with any other baboso in TJ. OKAY... I BELIEVE EVERYTHING AND I'M HAPPY AND IT WON'T HAPPEN AGAIN (with other chicas).

So now the fear of commitment (equal with hookers and non-hookers) shows its familiar face. "So why are you leaving me this weekend?"

"I have to go to Ensenada and Tecate."

(Actually, no, I fucking don't. I HAVE PLANS to go to Ensenada and Tecate, but nobody is counting on me being there.) But I go and leave her behind. *Que Imbécil!*

Naturally, if you're still with me on this thread, you're wondering along with me what the hell fueled all of this? Beyond a couple of easy/stupid romantic constructions that I fashioned under her direct questioning, and the fact that she probably wasn't accustomed to discussing Mexican politics and sociology over her ficha drink, I just can't say. She did ask me repeatedly before we got into action why I hadn't sought her out all week when I had been, as she well noted, alone.

Well, it is true that I patronized nobody else in CC that week, but it was overall about the least chaste week I've passed through in many a year. And so I told her that I was constructing the fantasy of being with her, that I was depriving myself of her and ALL female company (fucking scoundrel!) solely to build the time that we were about to have together to a crescendo of fantasy fulfillment.

And goddamn, I guess she believed me!!! Our lovemaking was only interrupted by her asking me to repeat this bullcrap over and over again, like a giddy little girl experiencing her own defloration and not like a new Mexicana at all. What I won't do to conjure a GFE, but when it was 20% done, I felt like she was my girlfriend. Hell, all of my constructs may as well have been fully sincere.

I'll see her again this weekend and hope she remembers my name. But not very many times following this weekend if her portrayals are really her life. She says she's resuming study and career opportunities back in the south of Mexico early next year, and will remain in TJ only until she heads for home for the holidays in December. So I've got two months, but will only be able to see her 2-3 more times at best as presently calculated. That may be just fine. Once again, fear of commitment. I suspect the symphony of last Thursday night would not have been as fully realized if I didn't believe that she is leaving town in December. I can see the beginning, middle and end. And so I am set free.

THREE WEEKS LATER

Here's a follow-up on the peculiar aftermath of my "deflowering" by the short-term chica at CC.

I have spent a number of nights with her since the initial spectacular. I never had an interest in being this chica's "novio", but clearly that first night presented a fork in the road where I could have steered to a no-pay but strings attached relationship with her, or moved comfortably back towards a commercial arrangement. I chose the latter and as I did, I believed that any extracurricular significance that our being together may have had, ebbed gradually but surely out of the picture.

In the end, this felt like a strictly commercial arrangement, but one in which I had been grandfathered into the intensity of the passion and sex we enjoyed on that magical first night. So the illusions were gone but we still rearranged all the dust in the room and there was still genuine personal warmth. This is what you want in TJ.

Commercial or not, given her very brief run in TJ and the quality companionship she provided, I did feel obligated at least to not go with other CC chicas while she is in town, a concession I've never made to any other AB or CC chica (other bars are a different story).

So I visited TJ this weekend for our last stand... happily so that it would be our last, that is. Really looking forward to returning to free agent status when she leaves town for good 1-2 weeks from now. At the conclusion of our last session, she told me she'd be leaving for her home state earlier than planned, but that she plans to visit me in LA in January (she has a tourist visa). I don't believe it, but the suspense won't last long.

Then she shocks me with the declaration that even though we will reside something like 1,800 miles apart, we will remain novios… that she expects I won't be dating other girls in LA, and she will likewise remain faithful.

Now we mongers get these games all the time from chicas who remain in TJ and are looking for that competitive edge, but what the fuck is up with her giving me the line when we can't even see each other and she is abandoning sex work very probably for good? (Yes, I believe she'll be the exception to the "they always come back" rule.) What exactly is she angling for? She has firm long-term plans in Mexico that don't involve any interest in US fiancée visas or anything like that. She is educated, independent, serious, qualified, connected and motivated towards career. What is her game in the best little whorehouse in Tijuana?

So I respond that following her visit to LA in January, that the next time we are likely to be in the same room together is at my funeral should she be kind enough to attend. I ask her if she now feels the need to re-virginize me after de-virginizing me only a month ago?

I was exhausted and didn't have the energy to translate/understand her response… didn't matter. Had to be nonsensical.

Much Later That Evening

Now having had an opportunity to truly decompress, I feel pretty stupid to even have reflected about this online. It now seems obvious that she's just one of a large number of people who are uncomfortable with confronting goodbyes straight on.

When I'm in the middle of a situation with a chica in Mexico, I tend to look at the communication more literally than I would with a gringa in a similar situation. The setting, the work involved for me in communicating about things that matter in Spanish, the misunderstandings inherent to cultural differences; all those contribute to place me as standing in cement when communicating with a TJ chica who has elevated the experience… whereas in another situation, I might be dancing gracefully through the folds of cryptic meaning.

It was dimwitted of me to have been puzzled by her pronouncements. Now I get it.

AT THE MERCY OF THE BEAST

KENDRICKS

I returned to Tijuana this weekend after what seemed an eternity. To my delight, very little had changed in my absence. Tijuana used to be an escape, but it has now become an anchor to my very tenuous grip on reality. The sensations of excitement and anticipation are always heightened by my constant longing to return. Always one to prolong my agony, I decided to hit a few Revolución Street strip clubs before my inevitable plunge into the underworld of the Zona Norte.

After enjoying a few bouncing titties at Peanuts & Beer and Pussycats, I wandered into the Beverly Hills Club, where I quickly pounced on a ringside seat. There was a decent crowd, but no dancer on the stage. A couple of drunken gringas abandoned their boyfriends to playfully dance on the stage until a beautiful morena pro strutted in between them.

The Azteca goddess immediately ripped off her own top, exposing her dark, beautiful, natural breasts. A professional like this knows what the boys came to see. She gracefully slithered behind one of the gringas and attempted to lift her top over her ample breasts.

But no! This little American tramp believes her breasts are too precious for a crowd of degenerates to gaze upon. She grabbed the bottom of her shirt, and pulled away from the beautiful young

Mexicana. The crowd was becoming restless, and I doubt I was the only man in the room who felt cheated by her obnoxious reluctance.

Moments later, the stripper had coaxed the other gringa to the floor. This girl was too drunk to put up much of a fight. Her dark skinned cousin quickly freed her breasts and ran her hands over the gringa's pussy while licking and sucking her chichis. Female flesh on female flesh is a beautiful sight indeed, and the young white girl seemed to be enjoying her part in the performance.

Her enjoyment faded as she finally made it to her feet and turned, half naked, to face a crowd of cheering men. Ecstasy turned to tears as she covered her precious milk bags and hurried back to her seat, shattered and on the verge of an emotional breakdown.

Was I the only man in the room to feel a vicarious thrill as her face contorted with shame and regret? By the sound of the applause and catcalls, my guess is I was not. I was now throbbing hard at this display of unwilling flesh, exposed for the world to see in all its drunken glory.

The beautiful morena smiled and continued her show. I wanted her in a very bad way. My skin was jumping from my body, and desire coursed through my veins. This little Mexican hottie had blood lust in her heart, and had no sympathy for the timid and the weak. What a woman!

I held a dollar in front of me, and she quickly took the bait. My face was soon filled with a blur of soft breasts and hard nipples as she jumped into my lap and ground her cunt onto my throbbing cock. Ecstasy and denial, pleasure and pain, love and lust, the desire to fuck and the thrill of seeing a stuck-up little bitch humiliated and destroyed overwhelmed my mind. But my dollar's worth of contact was quickly over with, and the predatory little diosa returned to her show.

I glanced back at the gringa, who was still sobbing with emotional pain. The shattered look in her eyes warmed my heart, and fueled my lust. The entire scene had crazed me with primal emotions, and I was dying for a release.

Once the set was over, I quickly grabbed this intense morena stripper for a private lapdance. I knew she would put me over the edge, and she did not disappoint.

(A girlfriend once told me she loved to suck cock, as this gave her incredible power over big, strong men who had previously looked at her as helpless and weak. She could completely control any man, so long as he was on his back, and her hot, wet mouth was bobbing on his excited tool. At that moment, there was nothing he would not say, nothing her would not promise her, in exchange for her completing the deed. Since she told me this between licks and slobbers on my throbbing rod, I could only moan my agreement as she proved her point.)

Inside the booth, the tight little morena stripper was down to her g-string in nothing flat and wasted no time in bringing my verga to full attention. Her soft, beautiful tits rubbed my face and were soon rubbing against my bare chest. She opened my pants, pulled my shirt down over my rock hard prick, and was soon grinding me to the point of no return.

Ever fiber of my being was dying to penetrate her, but I leaned back in the chair to allow the sweet torture to continue. She smiled devilishly as my hips bucked against hers, and my body hungrily rubbed against her sweet, soft breasts. She brutally continued the assault until I could no longer control myself, and was gushing cum underneath the driving force of her grinding panocha.

Once my orgasm was complete, she stood and ran her hands across the puddle of cum that soaked the front of my shirt. "Te gusta mi baile, sí, papi?" she laughed, before leaning over to softly kiss me. I can only hope that hell will be so sweet, when I make my final descent.

I was high on a rush of endorphins and emotions as I wandered from the booth. I smiled when the recently de-cloaked gringa bitch caught my eye and then returned her head to the table top, where it belonged.

What an amazing scene; I truly felt privileged to be part of such a moment in time. Only in Tijuana can such things happen in this Foul Year of Our Lord, 2003.

Perhaps I should have been ashamed of my cum soaked shirt as I strolled back through the club, but the thought never occurred to me. I wore it as a badge of honor, and I doubt I was the first semen-stained gringo to wander the streets of Tijuana. And I certainly will not be the last.

I drained another beer and pondered my next move. The light entertainment phase of my night was now over with; I had no choice but to venture back into the Zona Norte.

The night was too perfect to go up with just anyone. She had to be hot, she had to have a body to die for, and without a doubt, she had to be slutty as hell. After touring several clubs, I parted the red curtains of Adelita and hungrily prowled the aisles for my object of desire.

My quest did not take long. I knew she would be mine the moment I laid eyes upon her. She was dark and sweet, with painted-on eyebrows and heavy blue eyeshadow, killer tits tied up in a halter top, and a healthy, voluptuous body that sent blood rushing into my cock.

Skipping the formalities, I invited her to the room, on the condition that she would drive me wild. She smiled her agreement, grabbed my hand, and pulled me through the crowd.

I quickly shed my clothes in the room, my shaft standing at attention before she could even touch me. I moved to untie her halter, and my heart skipped a beat when she protested.

Fortunately, her only request was that the halter stay tied, and she immediately pulled the skimpy top to the side to free her glorious mammaries.

I pulled her onto the bed and handed her a banana-flavored

condom. She skillfully wrapped my tool and looked me in the eye as she ran her tongue along my shaft, and then sucked it into her mouth.

As much as I love blowjobs, I was dying to drive my cock inside of her. This time, it would be me who had the control, while she laid back and took what I was dishing out. I moved her onto her back, spread her legs, and spent a few seconds masturbating her cunt lips with my engorged rod. Moments later, I slid it in up to the hilt, moved myself on top of her body, and pressed her wrists down over her head.

She bucked and moaned as I penetrated her. The helpless look in her eyes was driving me wild, but there was no way in hell this was going to end quickly. This was going to last until I had savored every bit of her sweet, juicy flesh.

Sometimes a fuck is not just a fuck. When the stars are aligned just right, and the state of the cosmos has come together perfectly, a pussy can grip a cock so tightly, and a dick can be so pounding hard, that you can feel every inch or her tight, sweet canal in a way that blocks out all other sensory input. We no longer had names. We were no longer members of any so-called civilization. We were fucking beasts, the female offering herself up in total submission, while her male counterpart ravished her, dominated her, completely using every ounce of her being to satisfy his own primal urge.

I eventually freed one of her hands so I could feel her big, firm, heaving breasts, and she grabbed my ass to pull me even more tightly inside of her. She threw her head back and moaned loudly, while I drove my spear into her at an ever-quickening pace.

Finally I had completely lost control and allowed myself to be thrown over the cliff as I pounded my orgasm into her. She furiously rose her hips to meet my thrusts while we uncontrollably plunged over the peak, and collapsed into each others' arms.

Once upon a time, Tijuana was my escape from reality. Now,

the banal reality of life in Southern California has become my escape not only from the beast that lives within Tijuana's soul, but from the beast that lives within my own heart as well.

¡Feeeneeshed!

Acknowledgements

EDITORS

We would be remiss in our efforts if we didn't thank all the literally thousands of Amigos who shared their stories, thoughts, and adventures with TJAmigos. The raw honesty and open sharing from everyone made TJA a unique spot on the web to learn about Tijuana and the mongering community as a whole.

In particular, thanks to El Fanatico for getting the ball rolling with TJAmigos back in the summer of 2003, Burt, Sampson (our most prolific poster), and Zambooy who freshened up the look and kept the site happening until the nebulous SESTA-FOSTA legislation came in to being.

For current information on Tijuana and the nightlife scene, we recommend joining TijuanaTalk.net.

The stories that remain unpublished are many and perhaps there will be a Volume II, but for now,

¡ADIÓS, AMIGOS... STAY SAFE OUT THERE!

www.ingramcontent.com/pod-product-compliance
Lightning Source LLC
Chambersburg PA
CBHW031148020426
42333CB00013B/567